40 Days at the Foot of the Cross

A Gaze of Love from the Heart of Our Blessed Mother

40 Days at the Foot of the Cross

A Gaze of Love from the Heart of Our Blessed Mother

By

John Paul Thomas

My Catholic Life! Inc.

www.mycatholic.life

ISBN-13: 978-1537622941

ISBN-10:1537622943

SPECIAL ACKNOWLEDGMENTS

Many thanks to Gwen and Fr. Black for their hours of editing and input.

DEDICATION

To our Blessed Mother who stood at the foot of the Cross of our crucified Lord. Her love and devotion toward her Son is an icon of perfect love, a window into the greatest of virtues and an invitation to holiness. Our Blessed Mother invites us to share in her motherly gaze upon her Son. She also invites us to allow her to gaze upon the crosses of our own lives.

Dearest Mother Mary, we thank you for your tender care. Teach us to imitate the love in your heart which was poured out upon your Son on Calvary.

This book is also dedicated to my sister Ann and to my parents. Ann suffered greatly for many years before passing away in 2006. Her suffering taught me much about the Cross of Christ. My parents were also shining examples of love and devotion toward Ann and in many ways reflected the love that our Blessed Mother had for her suffering Son.

BY

"JOHN PAUL THOMAS"

"John Paul Thomas" is the pen name this priest has chosen in honor of the Apostles Saints John and Thomas and the great evangelist Saint Paul. This name also evokes the memory of the great Pope Saint John Paul II.

John is the beloved Apostle who sought out a deeply personal and intimate relationship with his Savior. Hopefully the writings in this book point us all to a deeply personal and intimate relationship with our God. May John be a model of this intimacy and love.

Thomas is also a beloved Apostle and close friend of Jesus but is well known for his lack of faith in Jesus' Resurrection. Though he ultimately entered into a profound faith crying out, "my Lord and my God," he is given to us as a model of our own weakness of faith. Thomas should inspire us to always return to faith when we realize we have doubted.

As a Pharisee, Paul severely persecuted the early Christian Church. However, after going through a powerful conversion, he went on to become the great evangelist to the gentiles, founding many new communities of believers and writing many letters contained in Sacred Scripture. His letters are deeply personal and reveal a shepherd's heart. He is a model for all as we seek to embrace our calling to spread the Gospel.

CONTENTS

INTRODUCTION

In writing to the Church in Galatia, Saint Paul said, "May I never boast except in the cross of our Lord Jesus Christ, through which the world has been crucified to me, and I to the world" (Galatians 6:14). Saint Paul had clearly come to a profound realization that the Cross of Christ must be the single focus of his life.

From a purely earthly perspective, the Cross doesn't make sense. What is the value of suffering and death? What is the value of the brutal treatment of the Son of God? How could such a horrific incident ever be seen as something good, let alone the single boast of one's life?

These are difficult questions, and from an earthly perspective alone, they are impossible to answer. But from the point of view of grace and truth, from the perspective of God Himself, the answer is that in the Cross all goodness is contained. The Cross is the throne of all grace and mercy and from it alone new life is poured forth. There is no other source of the transforming power of God than the Cross.

The mystery of the Cross is just that: a mystery. In fact, it is the most profound mystery. In the Cross we see the greatest horror transformed into the greatest good. We see death become the source of life. Suffering becomes the source of healing. Bondage becomes the source of freedom.

Only God, in His perfect wisdom and power, is capable of transforming such evil into pure grace. Only God can do what no human mind could ever fathom to save humanity, dying a cruel death.

This book, *40 Days at the Foot of the Cross*, was written as a daily devotional by which the reader is invited to prayerfully ponder this most profound mystery of our faith. You are invited to stand at the foot of the Cross and gaze at our crucified Lord in openness to the mystery of His suffering death. As you do, be assured that Jesus has much to teach you and reveal to you about your own suffering. His lessons will be ones taught by His own witness and saving act of love. You will be invited to enter into this act of sacrificial love and unite yourself more deeply with its power and truth.

The meditations in this book are presented from the perspective of the greatest disciple of our Lord: His own dear mother. Mother Mary was one who faced the Cross of her Son with perfect openness, faith, love and devotion. Her fidelity to her Son throughout His life was unwavering. As she stood before the Cross during those long three hours, her fidelity never ceased.

This devotional attempts to ponder what our Blessed Mother would have pondered during those three hours. What was she thinking as she stood there gazing at her own Child dying? What memories went through her mind? What emotions and feelings filled her heart as she watched this final act of love?

The Scriptures do not reveal much about the interior ponderings of our Blessed Mother during those three hours, but the Scriptures do reveal to us many encounters between this mother and Son. Since the Cross was the culmination of the life of both mother and Son, it's beautiful to bring to this moment of the Cross all the many experiences that these two shared throughout their earthly lives. It's inspiring to unite all that they did and said to this moment, since all was a preparation for this moment.

As you read through these meditations, try to do so in a prayerful setting. Allow yourself to be drawn into the mind and heart of our Blessed Mother and try to understand how she viewed her Son's Cross. As you do, bring also your own crosses in life and look at them from the perspective of this loving mother. Allow her gaze to penetrate your crosses and to reveal to you the importance of their complete embrace. Enter into this mystery with faith and allow that faith to unite you more fully with the Cross of Christ, so that, with Saint Paul, the Lord's Cross will become your central and single "boast" in life.

Structure of this Book

This book offers 40 days of reflection on the Cross of Christ through the eyes of our Blessed Mother. It is a book of meditation and prayer recommended for the following situations:

1) Use this book as a Lenten meditation so that you can gently and continually enter more deeply into the Cross. If you spend Lent carefully and prayerfully meditating on the pages of this book, Good Friday and Easter will take on a much greater significance. There are forty days in Lent, not counting Sundays or the Triduum (Good Friday through Holy Saturday). Counting Sundays and the Triduum, there are actually forty-six days from Ash Wednesday until Easter Sunday. Therefore, you may begin these daily meditations for Lent any time within the first six days of Lent so as to finish by Easter Sunday. The goal, however, is not to be scrupulous about when you start. The goal is to use these meditations in a way that helps you enter more deeply into the mystery of our Lord's Cross during Lent.

2) This book is also ideal for someone who has been burdened with a heavy cross of their own. Perhaps it is the death of a loved one, a broken family relationship, hardships with work or finances, physical

illness or any other heavy burden. By spending 40 days looking at the Cross of Christ, the reader will be invited to unite their own burdens to Christ's Cross and receive from Him the strength needed to press on with faith and hope.

3) Since the Cross of Christ is the central mystery of our faith, this book is a fruitful "retreat" for any time of year for the person who is willing to plunge deeper into their faith. The content of this book is challenging in that it invites the reader to gaze at the Crucifixion day after day for 40 days. This requires commitment, but for those who are willing, the fruit of these meditations will be abundant any time of year.

4) Perhaps you are making a weekend retreat and are looking for good material for meditation. Though it may not be helpful to read this book from cover to cover in one weekend, you may feel called to go through several meditations in one day. If that is the case, make sure you pause and reflect when something affects you.

5) Instead of 40 days in a row, this book would be a fruitful source of meditation for 40 weeks in a row. It could be used during a weekly holy hour of adoration at church or a set time of private prayer at home.

Stabat Mater (The Mother was Standing)

The following prayer may be used before each meditation from this book any time of year.

At the Cross her station keeping,
stood the mournful Mother weeping,
close to her Son to the last.

Through her heart, His sorrow sharing,
all His bitter anguish bearing,
now at length the sword has passed.

O how sad and sore distressed
was that Mother, highly blest,
of the sole-begotten One.

Christ above in torment hangs,
she beneath beholds the pangs
of her dying glorious Son.

Is there one who would not weep,
whelmed in miseries so deep,
Christ's dear Mother to behold?

Can the human heart refrain
from partaking in her pain,
in that Mother's pain untold?

For the sins of His own nation,
She saw Jesus wracked with torment,
All with scourges rent:

She beheld her tender Child,
Saw Him hang in desolation,
Till His spirit forth He sent.

O thou Mother! fount of love!
Touch my spirit from above,
make my heart with thine accord:

Make me feel as thou hast felt;
make my soul to glow and melt
with the love of Christ my Lord.

Holy Mother! pierce me through,
in my heart each wound renew
of my Savior crucified:

Let me share with thee His pain,
who for all my sins was slain,
who for me in torments died.

Let me mingle tears with thee,
mourning Him who mourned for me,
all the days that I may live:

By the Cross with thee to stay,
there with thee to weep and pray,
is all I ask of thee to give.

Virgin of all virgins blest!,
Listen to my fond request:
let me share thy grief divine;

Let me, to my latest breath,
in my body bear the death
of that dying Son of thine.

Wounded with His every wound,
steep my soul till it hath swooned,
in His very Blood away;

Be to me, O Virgin, nigh,
lest in flames I burn and die,
in His awful Judgment Day.

Christ, when Thou shalt call me hence,
be Thy Mother my defense,
be Thy Cross my victory;

While my body here decays,
may my soul Thy goodness praise,
Safe in Paradise with Thee.

Translation by Edward Caswall, *Lyra Catholica* (1849)

Prayer for a Fruitful Lent

The following prayer may be used after each meditation from this book when it is used during the forty days of Lent.

My precious and crucified Lord, I offer You this Lent.
I offer it to You with total abandonment and trust.
I offer You my prayers, sacrifices and my very life this day.
Do with me, Lord, as You will.

I pray that this Lent will be fruitful.
I know You have much to say to me and much to do in my life.
May this Lent be a time through which Your mercy is poured in abundance into my soul,
and into the souls of all Your faithful.

Dearest Lord, help me to especially see my sins, this Lent.
Humble me so that I may see clearly.
Give me courage and strength to confess my sins,
and to turn from them with all my heart.

Enlighten me with Your Holy Word, dear Lord.
Help me to come to know You and to deepen the gift of faith in my life.
Show me the plan You have for me,
and place my feet upon the path You have chosen.

My suffering Lord, I thank You for the fullness of Your perfect Sacrifice.
I thank You for holding nothing back,
giving Your life to the last drop of blood.
May I offer You my very life as a sacrifice,
trusting in Your mercy with every offering.

Keep me faithful to my Lenten promises,
and bring forth new life through these sacrifices of love.
Strengthen my prayer and make me holy.
Help me to turn to You, each day,
seeking Your sacred and pierced Heart.

Blessed Mother,
you stood by your Son in His suffering and death,
stand by me, I pray, as I journey through this life.
Pray for me and offer me to Your Son,
that He may take me into His loving embrace.

Lord, Jesus, Son of the Living God,
have mercy on me a sinner.
Lord, Jesus, Son of the Living God,
have mercy on me a sinner.
Lord, Jesus, Son of the Living God,
have mercy on me a sinner.

Mother Mary, Mother of our Crucified Lord,
pray for us who have recourse to thee. Amen

Prayer to Trust in Divine Mercy

The following prayer may be prayed after each daily meditation any time of the year.

Most merciful Jesus,
I turn to You in my need.
You are worthy of my complete trust.
You are faithful in all things.
When my life is filled with confusion, give me clarity and faith.
When I am tempted to despair, fill my soul with hope.

Most merciful Jesus,
I trust You in all things.
I trust in Your perfect plan for my life.
I trust You when I cannot comprehend Your divine Will.
I trust You when all feels lost.
Jesus, I trust You more than I trust myself.

Most merciful Jesus,
You are all-knowing.
Nothing is beyond Your sight.
You are all-loving.
Nothing in my life is beyond Your concern.
You are all-powerful.
Nothing is beyond Your grace.

Most merciful Jesus,
I trust in You,
I trust in You,
I trust in You.

May I trust You always and in all things.
May I daily surrender to Your Divine Mercy.
Most Blessed Virgin Mary, Mother of Mercy,
Pray for us as we turn to you in our need.

Day One – A Mother's Love

> Standing by the cross of Jesus were his mother and his mother's sister, Mary the wife of Clopas, and Mary of Magdala. John 19:25

This is one of the most widely depicted scenes in sacred art throughout the centuries. It's the image of the Mother of Jesus standing at the foot of the Cross with two other women. Saint John, the beloved disciple, was also there with them.

This scene is far more than merely an image of the salvation of the world. It is more than the Son of God offering His life for us all. It is more than the greatest act of sacrificial love ever known to the world. It is so much more.

What else does this scene depict? It depicts the most tender love of a human mother as she stands gazing at her own dear Son, dying a horrific death and agonizing with the greatest suffering. Yes, Mary is the Mother of God and Jesus is the Son of God. She is the Immaculate Conception, conceived without sin, and He is the Second Person of the Most Holy Trinity. But He is also her Son and she is also His mother. Thus, this scene is deeply personal, intimate and familial.

Try to imagine the human emotion and experience that both mother and Son endured at this moment. Imagine the pain and suffering in the heart of the mother as she stood gazing upon the brutal treatment of her own Child whom she raised, loved and cared for throughout His life. Jesus was not only the Savior of the World to her. He was her own flesh and blood.

Reflect, today, upon one aspect of this sacred scene. Look at the human bond of this mother and her Son. Set aside, momentarily, the divinity of the Son and the immaculate nature of the mother. Look only upon the human bond they share. She is His mother. He is her Son. Ponder this bond today. As you do, try to let this glimpse penetrate your own heart so that you can begin to feel the love that they shared.

Dearest Mother, you stood at the foot of the Cross of your Son. Though He was God, He was first your Son. You bore Him, raised Him, cared for Him and loved Him throughout His human life. Then, you stood gazing at His bruised and beaten body.

Dearest Mother, you invite me into this mystery of your love for your Son, this day. You invite me to stand by you as you stood by your Son. I accept this invitation. The mystery and depth of your love for your Son is beyond comprehension. But, nonetheless, I accept your invitation to join you in this gaze of love.

Precious Lord, Jesus, I see You, gaze upon You and love You. As I begin this journey with You and Your dear mother, help me to begin on a human level. Help me to begin seeing all that You and Your mother shared. I accept Your profound invitation to enter into the mystery of this holy and human love.

Mother Mary, pray for us. Jesus, I trust in You.

Day Two – The Strength of the Immaculate Heart

> Standing by the cross of Jesus were his mother and his mother's sister, Mary the wife of Clopas, and Mary of Magdala. John 19:25

Again, today, we look at this most sacred scene of the Mother of Jesus standing at the foot of the Cross. Note that John's Gospel says she was "standing."

There is little doubt that the human emotion Mother Mary felt was extreme and intense. Her heart was broken and pierced as she gazed upon her dear Son hanging upon the Cross. But as she gazed upon Him, she stood.

The fact that she stood is significant. It is a small and subtle way by which this Gospel passage depicts her strength in the midst of great personal pain. Nothing could be more devastating than for her to witness such brutality toward the one whom she loved with her whole heart. Yet, in the midst of this excruciating pain, she did not give in to her grief or fall into despair. She stood, with the utmost strength, faithfully fulfilling a mother's love until the end.

Our Blessed Mother's strength at the foot of the Cross is rooted in a heart that is immaculate in every way. Her heart was immaculate in love, perfectly strong, perfectly faithful, unwavering in determination, and imbued with unfailing hope in the midst of earthly chaos. From the perspective of the world, the greatest tragedy possible was befalling her Son. But from the perspective of Heaven, she was being invited at the same moment to manifest the pure love of her Immaculate Heart.

Only a heart that loved with perfection could be so strong. The hope, in particular, that would have been alive within her heart was awe-inspiring and glorious. How does one have hope and strength like this in the face of such pain? There is only one way and it is the way of love. The pure and holy love in the Immaculate Heart of our Blessed Mother was perfect.

Reflect, today, upon the strength of the heart of our Blessed Mother. Gaze upon the love she had for her Son and allow yourself to be drawn into awe of this pure and holy love. When you find pain in your life to be intense and overwhelming, remember the love in the heart of this mother. Pray that her heart will inspire yours and that her strength will become your strength as you seek to face the crosses and hardships of life.

My most loving Mother, draw me into the purity and strength of your heart. You stood at the foot of the Cross, gazing upon your Son as He was so cruelly treated. Invite me into your heart of perfect love, so that I may be inspired by you and strengthened by your glorious witness.

My dear Mother, as you stood at the foot of the Cross, you set an example for all people. There is no better place to be than the foot of the Cross. Help me to never turn away from the Cross, hiding in fear, pain or despair. Free me from my weakness and pray for me that I may imitate the strength of the love of your heart.

Precious Lord, as You hung upon the Cross, You allowed the love of Your Heart to unite with the heart of Your mother. Invite me into this shared love, so that I may also be united with You in Your pain and suffering. May I never take my eyes off of You, dear Lord.

Mother Mary, pray for us. Jesus, I trust in You.

Day Three – The Thoughts of the Mother of God

> Standing by the cross of Jesus were his mother and his mother's sister, Mary the wife of Clopas, and Mary of Magdala. John 19:25

What was going through the mind of Mother Mary as she stood at the foot of the Cross gazing upon her crucified Son? What was she thinking?

Most people experiencing such persecution would encounter thoughts of confusion, anger and denial. Such encounters are very difficult to understand and the temptation to irrational and confused thinking would be strong. So what was going through the mind of our Blessed Mother?

Mother Mary not only had an Immaculate Heart, she also had a mind that was sharpened with the perfection of faith. In her faith she may not have had the same knowledge and understanding as she has now in Heaven, but her faith was such that she knew this horror was permitted by the will of the Father. Her mind would have grasped the deepest truth that her Son was fulfilling His divine mission. She would have known that this tragedy was not a tragedy at all; rather, it was the greatest act of love ever known.

Mother Mary's faith would have mixed with the pain she felt in that moment. Her faith would have been a source of great confidence as she was tempted to despair. Her faith would have transformed all temptations into clarity and conviction. In the end, she would have conquered her temptations by the truth revealed to her from the mind of God.

In our own lives, suffering leaves us confused and uncertain. It tempts us to lose faith and to doubt the perfect will of the Father in Heaven. We must learn from the witness of our Blessed Mother as she allowed the truth to direct her thinking as she faced her Son's suffering. Only the truth could set her free to understand and shed every temptation to doubt the wisdom of God.

Reflect, today, upon the perfect faith of our Blessed Mother. Her faith was an absolutely certain knowledge that God was in control and that the will of the Father was being achieved before her very eyes. Worldly wisdom was left with an impossible task of making sense of such cruelty. But Heavenly wisdom took over as she consented to the death of her Son for the salvation of the World.

Dear Mother, so many times in life I am tempted to doubt the ways of God. My own crosses, and those of my loved ones, can leave me confused. Pray for me that I may have your perfect faith as I go through this world of suffering and pain. May I never be deterred by the temptations that come from worldly wisdom alone, but instead allow the truth of Heavenly wisdom to flood my mind and give direction to my life.

Precious Jesus, You allowed Your Immaculate Mother to witness the excruciating pain of Your Cross. But You also bestowed upon her Heavenly insight and knowledge so as to help bring clarity to her mind. Pour forth this same knowledge upon me and upon all mankind. Help us to know You and Your perfect will in all things.

Mother Mary, pray for us. Jesus, I trust in You.

Day Four – Spiritual Friendship

> Standing by the cross of Jesus were his mother and his mother's sister, Mary the wife of Clopas, and Mary of Magdala. John 19:25

By the providence and will of God, our Blessed Mother was not at the foot of the Cross alone. She was joined by two other holy women as well as by Saint John the Apostle. Together they stood at the foot of the sacrifice of Jesus.

The strength of our Blessed Mother was unmatched. She and she alone could have stood at the foot of the Cross gazing in faith and perfect trust as she watched her Son endure His sacrifice. However, it was the will of the Father in Heaven that she not endure this alone. She was given certain spiritual companions with whom she would walk through this suffering.

In many ways, our Blessed Mother was more of a pillar of strength for her companions than they were for her. But we can also be certain that she allowed the companionship of Saint John and these holy women to bring comfort and strength to her own heart.

It is not the will of God that we face the hardships of life alone. Even if we were as strong and immaculate as our Blessed Mother, we could still be certain that God would want us to face the challenges of life with the assistance and consolation of others. Human life is made for communion with one another. Offering and receiving strength and consolation makes up part of who we are. Therefore, we must allow this holy scene at the foot of the cross to remind us of our need for the spiritual friendship of others. We must daily seek to embrace those friendships that God has given us and be open to new ones that He sends our way.

Reflect, today, upon two things. First, reflect in gratitude upon the people in your life who act as a source of strength and support in times of need. No one but Jesus and our Blessed Mother will be a perfect support, but if we are open, we will come to realize that there are many whom God uses to offer us strength and support in various ways. Reflect, also, upon those who need your spiritual friendship. Who has God placed on your heart to reach out to and to console? Stand with them, at the foot of their daily crosses, and together you will be gazing at our Lord Himself.

Dearest Mother, as you stood at the foot of the Cross you were joined by Saint John and the holy women. You allowed them to be a source of consolation to you who were immaculate in every way. You invited them into your own grieving heart and allowed their mutual love of your Son to bring you joy and strength.

Dear Mother, draw me also close to your heart. May I also become a spiritual consolation to you in this agony. As I do so, I trust that this closeness to you will also be a source of consolation to me in my suffering and pain. I thank you for standing by me throughout life and I renew my trust in your motherly care.

My dear Jesus, you draw me to Yourself and invite me to gaze upon You in Your agony. As I do so, give me the grace of true friends who will join me in my gaze of love towards you. May these friends strengthen me and may I always provide consolation to those in need.

Mother Mary, pray for us. Jesus, I trust in You.

Day Five – Total Surrender

> "Behold, I am the handmaid of the Lord. May it be done to me according to your word." Luke 1:38a

> "Father, if you are willing, take this cup away from me; still, not my will but yours be done." Luke 22:42

Our Blessed Mother always said, "Yes." This "Yes" was her *fiat* of perfect love. At the Annunciation, the Archangel Gabriel revealed to her the beginnings of the life of the Savior of the World. The Archangel revealed that she would be His mother and He her Son. Our Blessed Mother inquired with openness and submitted without reserve.

Mother Mary's *fiat* resounded throughout her life. Though faced with the great mystery of the Incarnation, she submitted with free and total consent to the will of God. As a result, God became one of us, incarnate in her immaculate womb.

Though her Son was God and was perfect in every way, He chose to imitate her perfect *fiat* as He agonized in the Garden of Gethsemane. That night, just hours before His brutal Crucifixion, He fell on His knees and cried out, "Father, if you are willing, take this cup away from me; still, not my will but yours be done." His prayer was one of perfect surrender to the will of the Father in Heaven. But it was more than that. His prayer also united Him ever more deeply to His own beloved mother. This prayer in the garden echoed Mary's *fiat* to the Father at the Annunciation. Just as His mother had said "Yes" to the will of God, so did her Son the night before He died.

As our Blessed Mother stood at the foot of the Cross, she would have pondered the union of her *fiat* with that of her Son. She would have seen that this moment was the culmination of their united surrender to the will of the Father.

Reflect, today, upon your own surrender to God. Say with Jesus and our Blessed Mother, "Let it be done unto me according to your word." And, "Not my will but yours be done." Pray these prayers and know that you are saying "Yes" to the Cross. By entering into this great mystery of our faith, you are offering your life in union with the Son and His mother. Do not hesitate. Offer yourself freely and you will be blessed to be at the foot of the Cross, gazing at our Lord with our Blessed Mother.

Dearest Mother, as you stood at the foot of the Cross and recalled your own perfect "Yes" to the will of the Father, you became immediately aware of what that "Yes" truly meant. It meant total sacrifice, surrender and death to all in this world. It meant you believed in the will of the Father above all earthly goods. It meant you chose to trust at a depth divine grace alone could make possible.

Draw me in, dear Mother, to your perfect fiat. *Help me to say those words with you as I face the mysteries, hardships, crosses and sufferings of my life. Give me the vision of your faith so that I may have hope and trust in all things.*

My Precious Lord, I choose to live Your perfect surrender and to make it my own. Grant me the grace to be one with You as You were one with the Father in Heaven and one with Your own dear mother. I love You, my Lord, and I give myself to You without reserve. Let it be done to me according to Your most holy will.

Mother Mary, pray for us. Jesus, I trust in You.

Day Six – A Leap of Joy Remembered

> When Elizabeth heard Mary's greeting, the infant leaped in her womb, and Elizabeth, filled with the holy Spirit, cried out in a loud voice and said, "Most blessed are you among women, and blessed is the fruit of your womb. And how does this happen to me, that the mother of my Lord should come to me? For at the moment the sound of your greeting reached my ears, the infant in my womb leaped for joy. Blessed are you who believed that what was spoken to you by the Lord would be fulfilled." Luke 1:41-45

As our Blessed Mother stood before the Cross of her Son, she had three long hours to ponder all the powerful moments and experiences of His earthly life. Perhaps her mind would have gone back to the beginning when Saint John the Baptist testified to Jesus from the womb of Elizabeth.

Saint John sensed the presence of the Savior of the World. He was not able to understand this mystery fully with his mind, but he understood the mystery in his spirit. Joy touched him and he leaped. This was not a willful response on his part, it was an inspiration from the Holy Spirit. He received this gift of joy and responded from within the womb. Elizabeth sensed that joy and she expressed it to the Mother of God and to all of us.

As our Blessed Mother gazed upon her crucified Son, the joy of that moment, experienced so many years ago, would have brought her peace and consolation. The Father had not abandoned her Son on the Cross. How could He? How could the Father and the Holy Spirit be absent from this moment? It was the Holy Spirit who inspired Saint John all those years ago with joy, and now it was the Holy Spirit, once again, who was inspiring Jesus' mother with a joy that transcended even her Son's death.

As Mother Mary gazed upon her crucified Son, her joy would have resulted from the simple fact that she was gazing upon her Son. She saw His divine soul under the veil of blood and bruises. Despite the horror of the Crucifixion, the joy of His Incarnation could never be erased. He was God and He was also her Son, her flesh and blood. What a joy, what a blessing, what a gift!

Reflect, today, upon the fact that God is present to you always, no matter what you go through in life. Even in the midst of the greatest sufferings, God is present. His presence is worth rejoicing over. This joy overshadows anything and everything we encounter in life. Let the joy of the presence of God enter your heart this day as you gaze, with our Blessed Mother, upon the suffering of the Son of God.

Dearest Mother, your eyes beheld the greatest horror ever known but your heart leaped for joy. The joy you felt was a result of the holy and simple fact that no matter what they did to your Son, He was still God and He was still your Son. His presence always inspired hope and joy and nothing could ever take that away.

Dear Mother, pray for me that I may keep my eyes on the divine presence of your Son, no matter what I endure in life. May that divine presence be the joy that enables me to rejoice always.

My most precious Savior, no matter how beaten and bruised You are, I rejoice in Your divine presence in my life. I rejoice in Your Incarnation and union with me. May I never allow the joy of Your presence to be overshadowed by the sufferings of life.

Pray for me, dear Mother. Jesus, I trust in You.

Day Seven – A Lowly Servant of the Lord

> "My soul proclaims the greatness of the Lord; my spirit rejoices in God my savior. For he has looked upon his handmaid's lowliness; behold, from now on will all ages call me blessed." Luke 1:46-48

As our Blessed Mother stood before the Cross of her Son, would "all ages" call that a "blessed" moment? Was she blessed, as she says in her song of praise, to behold the cruel and brutal death of her Son?

Though her experience at the foot of the Cross would have been one of exceptional pain, sorrow and sacrifice, it was also a moment of exceptional blessing. That moment, while she stood gazing with love at her crucified Son, was a moment of extraordinary grace. It was a moment through which the world was redeemed by suffering. And she chose to witness this perfect sacrifice of love with her own eyes and to ponder it with her own heart. She chose to rejoice in a God who could bring forth so much good from so much pain.

In our own lives, when we face struggles and suffering, we are easily tempted to turn in on ourselves in hurt and despair. We can easily lose sight of the blessings we have been given in life. The Father did not impose pain and suffering upon His Son and our Blessed Mother, but it was His will that they enter into this moment of great persecution. Jesus entered into this moment so as to transform it and redeem all suffering. Our Blessed Mother chose to enter into this moment so as to be the first and greatest witness to the love and power of God alive in her Son. The Father also daily invites each one of us to rejoice with our Blessed Mother as we are invited to stand and face the Cross.

Though the Scripture passage cited above recalls words our Blessed Mother spoke while she was pregnant with Jesus and went to meet Elizabeth, they are words that would have continually been on her lips. She would have proclaimed the greatness of the Lord, rejoiced in God her Savior and savored her numerous blessings in life over and over again. She would have done so in moments like the Visitation, and she would have done so in moments like the Crucifixion.

Reflect, today, upon the words and the heart of our Blessed Mother. Speak these words in your own prayer today. Say them within the context of whatever you are going through in life. Let them become a daily source of your faith and hope in God. Proclaim the greatness of the Lord, rejoice in God your Savior, and know that God's blessings are abundant every day no matter what you experience in life. When life is consoling, see the blessing in it. When life is painful, see the blessing in it. Allow the witness of the Mother of God to inspire you each and every day of your life.

Dearest Mother, your words spoken at the Visitation, proclaiming the greatness of God, are words pouring forth from the great joy of the Incarnation. This joy of yours extends far and wide and filled you with strength as you later stood watching your Child die a brutal death. The joy of your pregnancy touched you, once again, in this moment of deepest sorrow.

Dearest Mother, help me to imitate your song of praise in my own life. Help me to see God's blessings in every aspect of life. Draw me into your own gaze of love to see the glory of the sacrifice of your own beloved Son.

My precious Lord Jesus, You are the greatest blessing in this world. You are all blessings! Everything good comes from You. Help me to fix my eyes upon You each and every day and to be made fully aware of the power of Your Sacrifice of Love. May I rejoice in this gift and always proclaim Your greatness.

Mother Mary, pray for me. Jesus, I trust in You.

Day Eight – Fidelity in All Things

> Mary remained with [Elizabeth] about three months and then returned to her home. Luke 1:56

One beautiful quality that our Blessed Mother had to perfection was fidelity. This fidelity toward her Son was first manifested in her fidelity to Elizabeth.

Mother Mary was pregnant herself, yet she went to care for Elizabeth during her own pregnancy. She dedicated three months of her time doing what she could to make the last months of Elizabeth's pregnancy comfortable. She would have been there to listen, to understand, to offer advice, to serve and to simply express that she cared. Elizabeth would have been greatly blessed by the presence of the Mother of God during those three months.

The virtue of fidelity is especially strong in a mother. As Jesus was dying on the Cross, His dear mother would have been nowhere else except on Calvary. She spent three months with Elizabeth and the three long hours at the foot of the Cross. This manifested her great depth of commitment. She was unwavering in her love and faithful until the end.

Fidelity is a virtue that is demanded from each of us when we face the hardship of another. When we see others in need, suffering, sorrowful or persecuted, we must make a choice. We must either turn away in weakness and selfishness, or we must turn to them, bearing their crosses with them offering support and strength.

Reflect, today, upon the fidelity of our Blessed Mother. She was a faithful friend, relative, spouse and mother throughout her life. She never wavered in fulfilling her duty no matter how small or how great the burden. Reflect upon the ways that God is calling you to act with unwavering commitment toward another. Are you willing? Are you ready to come to another's aid without hesitation? Are you willing to understand their wounds, offering a compassionate heart? Seek to embrace and live this holy virtue of our Blessed Mother. Choose to reach out to those in need and to stand at the crosses of those you have been given to love.

Dearest Mother, your fidelity to Elizabeth during those three months set a beautiful example of care, concern and service. Help me to follow your example and to daily look for the opportunities I have been given to love those who are in need. May I be open to service in great and small ways and never waiver in my calling to love.

Dearest Mother, you were also faithful to the end as you stood with perfect fidelity before the Cross of your Son. It was your motherly heart that gave you the strength to stand and gaze at your beloved Son in His agony. May I never turn away from my crosses or the crosses that others carry. Pray for me that I may also be a shining example of faithful love to all who have been entrusted to my care.

My precious Lord, I commit to You with all my heart, soul, mind and strength. I commit to gazing upon You in Your agony and pain. Help me to also see You in others and in their sufferings. Help me to imitate the fidelity of Your own dear mother so that I may be a pillar of strength for those in need. I love You, my Lord. Help me to love You with all that I am.

Mother Mary, pray for me. Jesus, I trust in You.

Day Nine – Unwelcomed by the World

> While they were there, the time came for her to have her child, and she gave birth to her firstborn son. She wrapped him in swaddling clothes and laid him in a manger, because there was no room for them in the inn. Luke 2:6-7

One of the first great sorrows to fill the heart of our Blessed Mother came at the moment of Jesus' birth. It's hard to fathom that at the moment the Mother of God was about to give birth to her Son, the Savior of the World, the only place they were welcomed was a place where animals dwelt. There was no room for Him in the inn or in any other home. It must have been quite an experience for her. She was aware of the amazing fact that her Son was the promised Messiah. She knew that she had conceived Him miraculously, by the overshadowing of the Holy Spirit. But now that it was time to be born, He was rejected for the first time. His first bed was a manger, the feeding trough for animals.

Rejection was a part of the lives of Mary and Jesus. It began with His birth and ended on the Cross. Our Blessed Mother was there throughout. But the rejection they encountered in life never robbed them of their peace and joy. One thing that clearly overshadowed the rejection of the world was the shared love of this mother and Son. The bond that they shared served as their mutual daily spiritual food. Their shared love enabled them to overcome the pain of earthly rejection so as to live the will of the Father to perfection.

So often in life we also experience rejection, misunderstanding and a lack of welcome by the world. When this happens, there is a great temptation to get angry and even despair. The key to enduring rejection is to be certain of the love and full embrace of the Mother of God and Jesus her Son in your life.

They are always there with arms open wide. They will never leave you. They will never reject you.

This gift of their loving embrace must also be offered by you to others. You are called to be the Mother of Jesus and you are called to be Jesus Himself to others. Your care and concern for others must be motivated by the love you receive from this Holy Family.

Reflect, today, upon two things. First, know that you are always welcomed by the Mother of God and by Jesus her Son. You always belong to this family. Reflect, also, upon your duty to bring their family love to others. This is especially the case for those in need and those whom God has entrusted to your care. Do not waver in being welcoming in every way, for in the act of welcoming another, you will find that you are welcoming Christ Himself.

Dearest Mother, I thank you for welcoming me always as your child. May your heart be my home as I rest close to your Son. May I never be deterred by the rejection I encounter in this life. Instead, may I always turn to your loving embrace, knowing that you welcome me as you welcomed your Son into this world.

Help me, dear Mother, to always provide care to those who encounter rejection in this world. May I be an instrument of your welcoming heart to all who are in need.

Precious Lord, You had no place to lay Your head except a manger. Yet the presence of Your mother was all the welcome You needed. Help me to open my own arms to You as You show Yourself in others. Help me to seek out those rejected and in need. May I be that manger for them and a refuge of Your own divine love.

Mother Mary, pray for us. Jesus, I trust in You.

Day Ten – The Sword of Sorrow

> Simeon blessed them and said to Mary his
> "Behold, this child is destined for the fall and r.
> many in Israel, and to be a sign that will be
> contradicted (and you yourself a sword will pierce) so
> that the thoughts of many hearts may be revealed."
> Luke 2:34-35

As our Blessed Mother stood at the foot of the Cross, she would have pondered many moments from the past thirty-three years with her Son. One such moment was when she and Saint Joseph presented Jesus in the temple in accord with the Jewish custom.

As they brought their newborn child into the temple they were greeted by Simeon, a holy and righteous man who spent his days praying in the temple. Simeon had received a personal revelation from God that he would be blessed to see the Savior of the World before his own death.

When our Blessed Mother and Saint Joseph brought Jesus into the temple, Simeon was immediately aware that this Child was the promised Messiah. He took Jesus into his own arms and proclaimed:

> "Now, Master, you may let your servant go in peace,
> according to your word, for my eyes have seen your
> salvation, which you prepared in sight of all the
> peoples, a light for revelation to the Gentiles, and
> glory for your people Israel." Luke 2:29-32

He then turned to our Blessed Mother and spoke to her saying, "You yourself a sword will pierce."

The sword of sorrow, prophesied by Simeon some thirty-three years earlier in the temple, at Calvary pierced our Blessed Mother's heart. The Immaculate Heart of our Blessed Mother was deeply wounded with this promised sword as she stood at the foot of the Cross watching the cruelty befalling her Child.

One consolation that she would have received as this sword of sorrow pierced her heart so deeply was the recollection of this prophecy. The prophecy of Simeon would have clearly come to mind in this moment and the truthfulness of Simeon's words would have helped her to know that the sacrifice of her Son on the Cross was the fulfillment of His mission. Knowing this truth would have eased her pain as she gazed at the completion of the will of God.

We, too, are guaranteed various swords of sorrow in our lives. We are promised that if we follow Jesus we will also take up our crosses. We are promised that we will drink the same "cup" that He drank from, endure ridicule just as He did, and be called to give our lives in a sacrificial and total way. Knowing the truth of our calling in life helps us be at peace when the sacrificial aspects of our personal mission come to fruition.

Reflect, today, upon two aspects of this scene on Calvary. First, ponder the deeply painful sword of sorrow that our Blessed Mother endured as she stood before the Cross of her Son. Secondly, reflect upon the consolation she would have received as she recalled the words of Simeon the prophet. Pondering those words strengthened her and enabled her to see her Son's death as the fulfillment of the will of God. In turn, knowing the truth of your mission of sacrificial love will help you as you endure the swords of life.

Dear Mother, as you stood before your own divine Son on the Cross, the sword of sorrow prophesied by Simeon pierced your Immaculate Heart. Help me to see the pain in your heart this day. As I gaze upon this wound of love, help me to also see your heart's acceptance.

Dear Mother, may I hear the words of Simeon and accept them into my own life. In this life I am promised the same fate as you and your divine

Son. I am promised a life of sacrifice and suffering. But I am also given hope as I see sacrifice as the fulfillment of the will of God.

Dear Lord, help me to unite all suffering in life to You. May I accept the crosses I am given with hope, love and joy. May I never shy away from the fulfillment of Your will. I give myself to You, dear Lord, and pray that I may imitate Your total self-gift to the world.

Mother Mary, pray for me. Jesus, I trust in You.

Day Eleven – Living in Exile

> [B]ehold, the angel of the Lord appeared to Joseph in a dream and said, "Rise, take the child and his mother, flee to Egypt, and stay there until I tell you. Herod is going to search for the child to destroy him." Joseph rose and took the child and his mother by night and departed for Egypt. Matthew 2:13-14

As our Blessed Mother stood before the Cross of her Son, she would have recalled her flight into Egypt with Saint Joseph. They fled so as to protect Jesus from the brutality of Herod. But now that brutality had caught up with Him.

Perhaps Mother Mary wondered what Saint Joseph would have done this day if he were present. Would he have saved Jesus again by fleeing from Jerusalem? Would he have protected her Son from the evil that had befallen Him?

As she pondered these things, Mother Mary would have embraced the mystery of this suffering with full acceptance. They fled from Herod long ago because that was not His time. That was not the time for Jesus to give His life for the salvation of the world. But now His hour had come. Now all she could do was to stand in faith and trust as she was face to face with the great mystery of suffering.

In each of our lives there are moments to flee from suffering and pain and there are moments to embrace them. In some situations, God will protect us. In others He will invite us to fully embrace the cross we have been given.

As we gaze upon the Cross with Mother Mary, we should be aware of the perfect timing of the will of God. Jesus did not suffer before His time. The Father in Heaven protected Him from evil men until it was His moment of glory. This was His day. This was His hour. This was His moment to embrace sin and death.

Reflect, today, upon the timing of God in your own life. What is God calling you to embrace today? What cross is being given to you today? If the time is right and the day for your own cross has come, do not hesitate to embrace it. Do not look for a way out or for a place to escape. Face the Cross with Jesus and our Blessed Mother and know that you do so with their strength and support.

Dearest Mother, you were called to protect your Son throughout His life. You were called to be vigilant in your motherly care. Be my mother, this day, and cover me with your mantle of love. Free me from evil when God so wills it and always protect me from sin.

My Mother, when the time of my own suffering and cross arrives, help me to say "Yes" to that cross with confidence, knowing that you are standing right beside me.

My precious Lord, I know that You will always protect me from the evil one. Give me the grace to endure his malice and to do so with confidence and hope. May I keep my eyes upon You and Your glorious throne of the Cross. I love You, dear Lord. Help me to follow Your perfect example.

Mother Mary, pray for me. Jesus, I trust in You.

Day Twelve – A Shared Suffering

> When Herod realized that he had been deceived by the magi, he became furious. He ordered the massacre of all the boys in Bethlehem and its vicinity two years old and under, in accordance with the time he had ascertained from the magi. Matthew 2:16

Mother Mary was well aware of the fury of Herod. She was aware of the fact that countless innocent children suffered death on account of her own Son. She and Saint Joseph had fled to Egypt to protect Jesus, and when Herod found out, he issued orders for a massacre of all those precious children.

The evil that some are capable of is shocking and overwhelming. How could Herod do such a thing and how could he do so on account of Mary's own Son, Jesus? This massacre was the first clear sign to her that her life and that of her Son would be marked with suffering and pain.

But the martyrdom of those holy children should not leave us with shock and sorrow alone. We must look beyond their suffering and see their witness. They suffered on account of the Son of God. They were martyrs in the truest sense.

The suffering of those innocent children should teach us that the full embrace of suffering is a holy calling. This is especially the case when we are innocent in our suffering. So often, when we encounter the malice of another, we tend to revolt, get angry and rebel as we profess the injustice inflicted upon us. But this is not what these innocent martyrs did.

Many years later, as Mother Mary stood before the Cross of her Son, she would have been aware of His full and willing embrace of martyrdom. What He was saved from many years before was now coming to fruition. She would have pondered the deaths of those innocent children so long ago as she pondered the freely embraced sacrifice of her Son on the Cross.

Reflect, today, upon the difficult truth that you are called to give witness to Christ. You are called to give witness by embracing every form of unjust suffering you endure in life. You are called to embrace it freely, without anger and without opposition. Seek to understand the form of martyrdom that our Lord is calling you to embrace. As you do, rejoice that you are counted worthy to share in such a glorious witness.

Dearest Mother, your strength is glorious. You witnessed so much brutality in your life, yet you never wavered in faith. Your martyrdom was martyrdom in spirit and it was the result of your unwavering love.

Help me, dear Mother, to never give in to anger or despair as I see the evil of the world around me. Help me to remain steadfast in faith and in hope, trusting always in your motherly intercession.

Dear Lord, You allowed the innocent to suffer on account of Your own presence in the world. When You allow me to suffer, give me the strength and grace I need to accept these martyrdoms with confidence and hope. May I follow Your own glorious example and that of those holy innocents.

Mother Mary, pray for me. Jesus, I trust in You.

Day Thirteen – A Mother's Ponderings

> When his parents saw him, they were astonished, and his mother said to him, "Son, why have you done this to us? Your father and I have been looking for you with great anxiety." And he said to them, "Why were you looking for me? Did you not know that I must be in my Father's house?" But they did not understand what he said to them. He went down with them and came to Nazareth, and was obedient to them; and his mother kept all these things in her heart. Luke 2:48-51

As our Blessed Mother stood at the foot of the Cross, she may have recalled that time when Jesus, at age twelve, stayed behind in Jerusalem for three days. Our Blessed Mother and Saint Joseph returned to Jerusalem and searched diligently for Jesus. Finally, they found Him in the temple with the teachers and religious leaders.

At that time, while the Child Jesus was among the teachers of Israel, they were greatly impressed by Him. He asked them deep and probing questions and manifested a wisdom beyond His years. Scripture says that "all who heard him were astounded at his understanding and his answers" (Luke 2:47). Painfully, just two decades later, Our Blessed Mother watched these same religious leaders question her Son over and over again. During those three years of His public ministry, Our Blessed Mother saw that the religious leaders turned on her Son, seeking to trap Him, accuse Him and discredit His profound wisdom. What a difference the years had made. What they thought was interesting coming from a twelve year old, they interpreted as threatening coming from a thirty year old. The religious leaders now were jealous and envious. And it was primarily on account of their new malice that she was standing before her crucified Son, gazing at Him as He offered the sacrifice of His human life.

In our own lives, we may find that people turn on us as we grow closer to our Lord and our Blessed Mother. We should expect nothing less than the same treatment that Jesus received. People who were once our friends will, at times, become our greatest persecutors.

Reflect, today, upon any experience you have had with those who have turned on you or betrayed you on account of your faith in Jesus. Though not everyone experiences this to the same degree as our Lord, when it is experienced it can be a source of confusion, hurt, anger and even despair. As our Blessed Mother watched the cruelty toward her Son unfold, she would have forgiven those religious leaders who treated Him this way. She would have shown mercy to them and prayed for them in the midst of her own suffering. We are called to do the same.

My dear Blessed Mother, when Jesus was only a Child, you were amazed at the reaction of the religious leaders in the temple as they listened to Him and were astonished by His wisdom. You also saw those same leaders turn on your Son during His public ministry. You watched their affection for Him turn into loathing and their amazement turn into jealousy.

My dear Mother, when I seek to act as an instrument of your Son and to speak His words of wisdom, not everyone accepts these words. Pray for me that I may always forgive and accept misunderstanding and ridicule with the same faith and hope that you had as you stood before the Cross.

Precious Lord Jesus, You never ceased proclaiming Your perfect wisdom and love to the world. Though many accepted Your words, many did not. Help me to know that I am called to follow in Your footsteps. Help me to never be scandalized or shaken by the persecution of myself or another. Keep me faithful to You and faithful to the proclamation of Your holy Word.

Mother Mary, pray for me. Jesus, I trust in You.

Day Fourteen – "Do Whatever He Tells You"

> When the wine ran short, the mother of Jesus said to him, "They have no wine." [And] Jesus said to her, "Woman, how does your concern affect me? My hour has not yet come." His mother said to the servers, "Do whatever he tells you." John 2:3-5

These words were spoken by our Blessed Mother at the first of Jesus' miracles: "Do whatever he tells you." They are profound and powerful words which can easily serve as the foundation of our spiritual lives.

If our Blessed Mother would have spoken anything to her Son at the foot of the Cross, what would she have said? Would she have spoken words of despair or confusion, pain or anger? No, she would have spoken the same words she spoke at the Wedding of Cana. But this time, rather than speaking these words to the servants, she would have spoken them to her Son. "My dear Son, whom I love with my whole heart, do whatever the Father in Heaven tells You."

Of course Jesus did not need this advice, but He desired to receive it from His mother anyway. He desired to hear His mother speak to Him these words of perfect love. In pondering these words once spoken at Cana, our Blessed Mother and her divine Son would have shared a deep union as they gazed at each other during His agony on the Cross. Mother and Son both knew that His death was the accomplishment of the greatest good ever known. They would have both known that the will of the Father in Heaven was perfect. They would have both longed for and embraced this holy will without reserve. And these words would have been on both of their hearts as they gazed at each other in silence:

"My dear mother, do whatever our Father tells you."

"My dear Son, do whatever Your Father in Heaven wills of You."

Reflect, today, upon these words and know that mother and Son speak them to you. No matter what you face in life, our Blessed Mother and her divine Son are inviting you into this glorious command of love and obedience. They are exhorting you to stay faithful through all struggles, in good times, in difficult ones, through pain and joy. No matter what you experience in life, these words must always resound within your mind and heart. "Do whatever He tells you." Do not hesitate to hear and embrace these holy words.

Dearest Mother, you offer words of perfect wisdom. You invite all of your dear children to embrace the perfect will of the Father in Heaven. These words are not spoken to me alone. They were first spoken to you in the depths of your heart. You, in turn, expressed this command of love to all whom you encountered. You silently spoke them, also, to your own divine Son.

My loving Mother, help me to listen to you speak these words to me. Help me, by the power of your prayers, to respond to this calling to embrace the perfect will of God in my life.

My Precious Jesus, I choose to do all that You command of me. I choose Your will without reserve and I know that You invite me to follow in Your footsteps. May I never be deterred by the hardships of the Cross, but be transformed by the power of Your perfect will.

Mother Mary, pray for me. Jesus, I trust in You.

Day Fifteen – Hearing and Observing the Word of God

> While he was speaking, a woman from the crowd called out and said to him, "Blessed is the womb that carried you and the breasts at which you nursed." He replied, "Rather, blessed are those who hear the word of God and observe it." Luke 11:27-28

During Jesus' public ministry, a woman in the crowd called out to Jesus, honoring His mother. Jesus corrected her in a way. But His correction was not one that diminished the blessedness of His mother. Rather, Jesus' words elevated the blessedness of His mother to a new level.

Who more than our Blessed Mother would daily "hear the word of God and observe it" with perfection? No one was more deserving of this elevation to blessedness than our Blessed Mother.

This truth was especially lived as she stood at the foot of the Cross, offering her Son to the Father with full knowledge of His saving sacrifice and with complete consent of her will. She, more than any other follower of her Son, understood the prophecies of old and embraced them with complete submission.

How about you? As you gaze at the Cross of Jesus, are you able to see your own life united to His on the Cross? Are you able to embrace the burdens of sacrifice and self-giving which God is calling you to live? Are you able to observe every command of love from God, no matter how much He asks of you? Are you able to "hear the word of God and observe it?"

Reflect, today, upon the true blessedness of the Mother of God. She fully embraced the word of God and observed it to perfection. As a result, she was blessed beyond measure. God also wishes to bless you in abundance. The only requirement of these blessings is openness to the word of God and its full embrace. Understanding and embracing the mystery of the Cross in your life is truly the richest source of the blessings of Heaven. Understand and embrace the Cross and you will be blessed with our Blessed Mother.

Dearest Mother, you allowed the mysteries of the suffering and death of your Son to penetrate your mind and elicit great faith. As you understood, you also assented. I thank you for your perfect witness and pray that I may follow your example.

My Mother, draw me into the blessings that were bestowed upon you by your Son. Help me to find great value in freely embracing the Cross. May I always see the Cross as the source of the greatest joys in life.

My suffering Lord, I gaze upon You with Your own mother and pray that I may see You as she sees You. I pray that I may understand the depth of love that motivated Your complete self-gift. Pour forth Your abundant blessings upon me as I seek to more fully enter into this mystery of Your life and sufferings. I do believe, dear Lord. Please help my moments of unbelief.

Mother Mary, pray for me. Jesus, I trust in You.

Day Sixteen – The Greatest of Miracles

> [Jesus] said, "Do not weep any longer, for she is not dead, but sleeping." And they ridiculed him, because they knew that she was dead. But he took her by the hand and called to her, "Child, arise!" Her breath returned and she immediately arose. He then directed that she should be given something to eat. Luke 8:52b-55

This was but one of the many miracles that Jesus performed. Our Blessed Mother witnessed Jesus' miracles throughout His public ministry. His first miracle, at the Wedding of Cana, was done at her request. After that, Jesus performed many more. The dead were raised, the multitudes were fed, demons were cast out, the blind and deaf were cured and so much more.

As our Blessed Mother stood at the foot of the Cross, she would have hoped for one more miracle. As she gazed at her Son, she heard the mockery of the scribes and elders as they said, "He saved others; he cannot save himself. So he is the king of Israel! Let him come down from the cross now, and we will believe in him" (Matthew 27:42). And though there were some who were hoping that Jesus would come down from the Cross and save Himself in an earthly way, the miracle that our Blessed Mother hoped for was far greater.

What miracle did she hope for as she gazed at the Crucifixion of her Son? She hoped that the saving grace of His perfect sacrifice would be poured forth on all people so as to wipe away their sins. She hoped that the very scribes, Pharisees and elders who mocked her Son would convert and be saved on account of His death. She hoped that the soldiers who nailed Him to the wood would come to see the power of His Cross and turn their lives over to her Son. The greatest miracle that our Blessed Mother hoped for at the foot of the Cross was the salvation of the world.

Like Mary, we too must seek the greatest good in our lives and in the lives of others. Though at times we can be selfish in our desires and hopes, we must push beyond this selfishness and seek the miracle that was the culmination of Jesus' life. We must seek our own eternal salvation and the salvation of all.

Reflect, today, upon the miraculous power of our divine Lord. He can raise the dead, heal the sick, feed the multitude and restore sight to the blind. But there is one thing that He cannot do. He cannot impose the grace of His saving sacrifice upon those who obstinately resist it. Commit yourself to total openness to this grace so that Jesus' greatest miracle may be accomplished more fully in your life and so that the hope in the heart of our Blessed Mother may be fulfilled.

My dear Mother, you witnessed so many miraculous events in the life and ministry of your Son. You saw Him raise the dead, heal the sick and cast out demons. As you stood before the Cross on which hung your only Son, you may have been tempted to despair. But in your perfect faith, you dismissed such temptations and hoped in the last and greatest miracle offered by your Son. You had perfect hope in the miracle of the salvation of the world.

My dear Mother, pray for me that I may be a recipient of this last and greatest miracle. Help me to open wide the door of my heart so that I may receive all that your Son offers me from the Cross.

My precious Lord, I thank You for this last and greatest act of Your life. I thank You for the grace poured forth from Your Cross for my salvation and that of the whole world. I open my life to You, dear Lord, and beg that I may receive all that You wish to bestow upon me. I love You, dear Lord. Help me to love You more. Mother Mary, pray for me. Jesus, I trust in You.

Day Seventeen – Entering into Jerusalem

> The very large crowd spread their cloaks on the road, while others cut branches from the trees and strewed them on the road. The crowds preceding him and those following kept crying out and saying: "Hosanna to the Son of David; blessed is he who comes in the name of the Lord; hosanna in the highest." Matthew 21:8-9

How wonderful that greeting was, just one week before, when Jesus entered into Jerusalem. He was greeted with much joy and exaltation. "Hosanna!" they cried out as they laid palm branches before Him. They treated Him as a king.

But now our Blessed Mother watched as her Son, the King of all Kings, mounted His glorious throne to distribute His grace and mercy upon the world. This was no earthly kingship. It was much greater. It was a Kingship of such spiritual power and authority that it superseded mere earthly strength. It was a Kingship dispensing salvation from the throne of the Cross.

The contrast between Palm Sunday and Good Friday was startling. Many were left in confusion. They were disillusioned as they saw Jesus' life deteriorate from a glorious welcome into Jerusalem to carrying a cross out of the same city just days later. But our Blessed Mother and our Lord Himself saw things much differently. Their pain was mixed with the utmost joy and peace at the mounting of His throne. They both knew that Jesus would be exalted for all eternity and that the echoes of "Hosanna!" would reverberate forever in Heaven.

Jesus' earthly death united Heaven and Earth. His Cross became the permanent bridge connecting, across all space and time, God the Father with all His children on Earth. Though Jesus' death was painful, the sorrowful heart of our Blessed Mother would have brought Him much comfort as she continually cried out in silent adoration of her Son. As she gazed at Him, her Immaculate Heart continually proclaimed, "My Son, You are the King of All, Hosanna to You, dear Son! Hosanna to You, my Lord, my Son and my King! Hosanna in the highest!"

Reflect, today, upon this glorious song of praise. "Hosanna in the highest!" Speak this song as you gaze, with our Blessed Mother, upon the crucifix. See the crucifix as the Throne of Grace. See Jesus as the King of all Kings. Look with faith and love and peer under the veil of the blood and bruises. See the King and give Him eternal glory.

My dearest Mother, your gaze of love upon your Son looked beyond the earthly sufferings He endured and saw the glory of that sacred moment. You saw His sacrifice for what it was. It was the greatest act of mercy ever known.

My dear Mother, as you gazed upon your tender Son with much love, so also invite me into that gaze. Help me to see the glory of the Cross in every cross I endure. Help me to unite all sufferings to the Cross of your Son and to continually cry out, with you, "Hosanna! Hosanna in the highest!"

My Suffering Lord, You are the Great King of All. Pour forth upon me and upon the whole world the abundant grace won by Your Cross. Fill my heart with hope and faith as I gaze upon You. Draw me close to Your throne now and for all eternity.

Mother Mary, pray for me. Jesus, I trust in You.

Day Eighteen – "This is My Body...This is My Blood"

> While they were eating, Jesus took bread, said the blessing, broke it, and giving it to his disciples said, "Take and eat; this is my body." Then he took a cup, gave thanks, and gave it to them, saying, "Drink from it, all of you, for this is my blood of the covenant, which will be shed on behalf of many for the forgiveness of sins." Matthew 26:26-28

The first celebration of the Most Holy Eucharist took place at the Last Supper when Jesus instituted both the Priesthood and the Holy Eucharist in the presence of His Apostles. The offering of this ritual Sacrifice culminated in His physical sacrifice upon the Cross, when He drank the bitter wine and exclaimed, "It is finished!" Our Blessed Mother witnessed this eternal outpouring as she stood at the foot of the Cross. As she did so, she adored every drop of His Precious Blood falling to the ground to sanctify the world.

After the Resurrection, our Blessed Mother was privileged to share in her Son's life in a new and profound way, every time she shared in the feast of the Holy Eucharist. She drank her Son's own Precious Blood and ate His Sacred Body as she joined the Apostles for the Holy Mass.

The image of the suffering and death of her Son was forever burned into her mind and stamped upon her heart. But the union she shared with Him through her reception of Holy Communion brought perfect clarity to His suffering and death. With every reception of His Body and Blood, she also received His Soul and Divinity. In this gift of the Eucharist, she experienced His closeness like never before and knew that His death on the Cross was the source of her new and profound union with Him. No longer was He someone whom she gazed at from a distance with love. No longer was He someone whom she carried only in her womb. He was now someone whom she consumed and thus entered into her own heart and soul in the deepest way.

As she gazed at Him and saw Him breathe His last, all earthly hope of being with Him was lost. But in that moment, as He cried out, "It is finished!", her relationship with her Son was forever changed. His life had been given back to God the Father, yet she was among the first to receive Him in the Holy Eucharist.

Reflect, today, upon the deep relationship that our Blessed Mother had with her Son. Her communion with Jesus reached a new and more profound level of love as she was privileged to receive Him into her body and soul in the Holy Eucharist. We too are all called to this same depth of communion with Jesus. We too are all invited to become one with Him as we partake of the gift of the Holy Mass. Reflect upon how deeply you believe in the presence of our Lord in this Sacrament. Reflect upon how completely you open yourself to the graces of this Gift. Recommit yourself to being consumed by our Lord as you consume His Body and Blood, Soul and Divinity. Know that the union you are called to live with Him is on account of His glorious gift of the Cross.

My loving Mother, as you gazed upon your Son you saw Him breathe His last. You watched Him die and offer His life for the salvation of the world. But you also saw so much more. As you saw His sacrifice come to completion, you also saw it transformed into a new beginning. You witnessed the beginning of the Most Holy Eucharist of which you were privileged to partake for the rest of your life.

My dear Mother, pray that I may have the grace of a faithful participation in the reception of the Body and Blood of your Son. May I, like you, receive Him with the utmost faith and allow His saving Sacrifice to consume every part of my soul.

My dear Lord, You gave us the Eucharist as the gift of Your continual presence among us. In this precious gift, You invite me to enter into communion with You on a profound level. As I gaze at Your Cross and see Your Blood poured out, help me to open my soul like a sponge soaking up Your divine presence. Unite Yourself with me, dear Lord, as I give myself to You.

Mother Mary, pray for me. Jesus, I trust in You.

Day Nineteen – The Agony in the Garden

> "My soul is sorrowful even to death. Remain here and keep watch with me." He advanced a little and fell prostrate in prayer, saying, "My Father, if it is possible, let this cup pass from me; yet, not as I will, but as you will." Matthew 26:38-39

> He was in such agony and he prayed so fervently that his sweat became like drops of blood falling on the ground. Luke 22:44

The agony that Jesus underwent while praying in the Garden of Gethsemane was only surpassed by the brutal treatment and Crucifixion He endured the following day. That Thursday night, after sharing the gift of His Body and Blood with the Apostles, He went out to pray. As He prayed, He fell prostrate before the Father in Heaven and accepted the "cup" that He was given to drink. Three times He prayed this profound prayer: "My Father, if it is possible, let this cup pass from me; yet, not as I will, but as you will."

That night would have been a sleepless one for our Blessed Mother. She was awoken in the middle of the night by the frightening news that Jesus had been arrested. She went in haste to the place of Jesus' interrogation before Caiaphas and the entire Sanhedrin, watching from a distance with the other holy women.

Jesus had agonized in the Garden and three times chosen the will of the Father. Saint Peter, during the commotion of the night, three times denied Jesus. Our Blessed Mother, during her silent presence throughout that night, united her mind and heart to the agony of her Son and to His free embrace of His Cross.

This was His Hour. This was The Hour in which Jesus was to give the greatest glory to the Father in Heaven. And it was also our Blessed Mother's hour. She was invited to freely offer her Son to the hands of evil men. Saint Peter and the other Apostles lacked fidelity and commitment as this hour approached. But our Blessed Mother, her Son's first and greatest disciple, joined Jesus in a complete surrender to the will of the Father.

On Good Friday, as Mother Mary stood before the Cross of her Son, she would have continued to pray in the way Jesus prayed in the Garden the night before. "Father...not as I will, but as you will." This must also become the most central prayer in our own lives each and every day.

Reflect, today, upon the chaos and confusion that began that night with Jesus' arrest. Reflect, also, upon moments of chaos and confusion in your own life. When you feel the burden of the various crosses in your life, there is but one way to properly embrace them. You must unite yourself with the prayer of Jesus in the Garden which was also the perfect prayer of our Blessed Mother. Join them in this prayer of perfect surrender.

Dearest Mother Mary, you watched in sorrow as your Son was arrested and treated with much cruelty. Yet your only prayer was the prayer your Son prayed in the Garden. "Father, not as I will, but as You will." Jesus' agony was your agony and His surrender was your surrender.

Pray for me, dear Mother, that I may join you and your Son in prayer as I agonize in this life. As I face the cruelty of the world, pray for me that I may also daily choose the will of the Father in all things, never giving in to despair and never wavering in my surrender.

My suffering Lord, I choose to stay awake with You and to remain faithful to You always. Give me the grace I need to live in complete surrender to the will of the Father and to Your most holy will.

Mother Mary, pray for me. Jesus, I trust in You.

Day Twenty – The Innocence of the Lamb of God

> So the band of soldiers, the tribune, and the Jewish guards seized Jesus, bound him, and brought him to Annas first. He was the father-in-law of Caiaphas, who was high priest that year. John 18:12-13

When Jesus was arrested, He was bound and led before Annas the high priest. Annas then sent Him to Caiaphas, who questioned Him, mocked Him and then sent Him to Pilate. Pilate then sent Jesus to Herod who questioned Him, ridiculed Him and then returned Him to Pilate. Jesus endured one interrogation after another.

After questioning Jesus, Pilate stated to the chief priests and to the crowds, "I find this man not guilty" (Luke 23:4). Herod also questioned Jesus and found Him "not guilty," sending Jesus back to Pilate. For a second time, Pilate addressed the chief priest and crowds saying, "You brought this man to me and accused him of inciting the people to revolt. I have conducted my investigation in your presence and have not found this man guilty of the charges you have brought against him, nor did Herod, for he sent him back to us. So no capital crime has been committed by him. Therefore I shall have him flogged and then release him" (Luke 23:14-16).

Jesus was innocent. That was the double verdict of both Herod and Pilate, even though Pilate eventually consented to Jesus' death. But the most important spiritual point is that Jesus *was* innocent. And it was precisely His innocence that made His death a sacrifice. If He had been guilty then His punishment would have been justified. But His innocence transformed His punishment into an atoning sacrifice for the salvation of the world.

As Our Blessed Mother listened to Pilate speak, proclaiming the innocence of her Son, she would have agreed with her whole heart. But she would have also understood that His innocence would not end in His earthly release. Rather, she would have understood well, as she listened to Pilate, that her Son was soon to become the innocent Lamb sacrificed for the sins of many. She would not have held on to an earthly hope for His release from these evil men. She would have held on to the hope that Jesus' innocent suffering and death would instead release all men from sin.

Reflect, today, upon the innocence of Jesus. "Though He was sinless, He suffered willingly for sinners. Though innocent, He accepted death to save the guilty" (Preface for Palm Sunday). It was our Lord's innocence that made His death the perfect sacrifice. Our Blessed Mother understood this well. As you ponder this truth, see the innocence of Jesus through the eyes of His Blessed Mother. Ponder her knowledge of His pure and perfect Heart. Reflect upon the gratitude and hope Mother Mary had as she stood before the Cross watching her innocent Son die for the salvation of the world. As she united her innocent heart with His, so you must unite your sinful heart to theirs, trusting that the sacrifice of the Lamb of God will take away all your sins.

My dear Mother, with the affection of your Immaculate Heart, you gazed at your Son in His innocence. You did not need to hear the words of Pilate to convince you of this truth. You knew His innocence better than anyone. But you also knew that His innocent suffering would become the source of salvation for all who would choose to accept this gift.

My dear Mother, I am guilty and deserve the death that your Son unjustly received. I am also eternally grateful for the freedom I have been given from my sins on account of Jesus' perfect sacrifice.

My innocent Lord, Your sacrifice was perfect and Your willing acceptance of the Cross is the source of salvation for all who will accept it. Give me the grace to open my soul to the gift of Your love and, in turn, to imitate Your innocent suffering by embracing the crosses and injustices that arise in my life's journey with faith and hope.

Mother Mary, pray for me. Jesus, I trust in You.

Day Twenty-One – The Scourging and Mockery

> Then he released Barabbas to them, but after he had Jesus scourged, he handed him over to be crucified. Then the soldiers of the governor took Jesus inside the praetorium and gathered the whole cohort around him. They stripped off his clothes and threw a scarlet military cloak about him. Weaving a crown out of thorns, they placed it on his head, and a reed in his right hand. And kneeling before him, they mocked him, saying, "Hail, King of the Jews!" They spat upon him and took the reed and kept striking him on the head. And when they had mocked him, they stripped him of the cloak, dressed him in his own clothes, and led him off to crucify him. Matthew 27:26-31

As Jesus was being scourged at the pillar, crowned with thorns and mocked by the soldiers, Mother Mary knew, with a mother's intuition, that her Son was suffering immensely. She suffered every lash, felt every thorn, and heard every vile word shouted at her precious Child.

Later that day, as she stood at the foot of the Cross, she would have recoiled at every wound in Jesus' torn flesh and every bruise on His sacred body. Yet she did not shy away from looking at her beaten Son with her motherly gaze. She needed to see the effects of the brutality Jesus had bravely endured. As she pondered the crown of thorns perched on His bloody scalp, she saw a true crown of grace and mercy.

How does a mother experience so much cruelty toward her own child and not be filled with hate? How does she not fall into despair and defeat? The answer is simple. This mother, the Mother of God, saw all things and experienced all things through her Immaculate Heart. Her love for her Son was so deep that it overflowed into the lives of those who beat Him and mocked Him. Love was the only option in the face of so much hate. She could only offer mercy as she and her Son absorbed hate and violence. All that evil was filtered through her Immaculate Heart until it was refined and poured out as mercy.

In our own lives, one of the most painful experiences we can bear is the mockery of another. To be laughed at, treated with contempt, ridiculed and disregarded is painful. It's "normal" to want to fight back. But we must seek to imitate the calm love in the heart of our Blessed Mother, never reciprocating hate for hate, evil for evil, and injury for injury.

Reflect, today, upon the feelings, thoughts and inner experiences of the Mother of God as she painfully witnessed the scourging and mockery of her Son. Enter into the stream of immaculate love that flowed from her heart, quenching the temptation toward hate. Reflect, especially, upon any ways that you have experienced the mistreatment of another. Know that our Blessed Mother also stands at this cross of yours, whether you have been mistreated or have yourself mistreated someone else, seeing all that you feel and experience. She stands at your side with a mother's love, her heart overflowing into yours.

My dearest Mother, I can only imagine what your heart must have felt as you gazed upon your Son in His broken and beaten state. I can only imagine the pain you felt as you adored every scourge and heard every mockery. But the love within your heart overshadowed every temptation toward anger and despair. Your love for your Son was immaculate and glorious.

My Immaculate Mother, I thank you for also being a faithful and loving mother to me. As I experience the crosses of my own life, I know you are there, standing by me, seeing and experiencing every wound I have. Thank you for your love and concern for me, your child. Help me to be open to the overflowing love in your heart so that this love may become my hope and my strength.

My scourged and mocked Jesus, though covered with wounds and surrounded by ridicule, You never gave in to hate. Your act of perfect acceptance of this abuse transformed sin into grace. Pour forth that grace upon me, dear Lord. Help me to turn to You in my times of need.

My dear Mother, pray for me. Jesus, I trust in You.

Day Twenty-Two – "Behold, Your King!"

> Consequently, Pilate tried to release him; but the Jews cried out, "If you release him, you are not a Friend of Caesar. Everyone who makes himself a king opposes Caesar."

> When Pilate heard these words he brought Jesus out and seated him on the judge's bench in the place called Stone Pavement, in Hebrew, Gabbatha. It was preparation day for Passover, and it was about noon. And he said to the Jews, "Behold, your king!" They cried out, "Take him away, take him away! Crucify him!" Pilate said to them, "Shall I crucify your king?" The chief priests answered, "We have no king but Caesar." Then he handed him over to them to be crucified. John 19:12-16

Yes, Jesus was the King of Kings and the Lord of Lords. Our Blessed Mother knew this truth deep in her heart. Therefore, as she watched Pilate bring her beaten and bruised Son out for all to see, and then proclaim Him as King, she would have heard and believed. Pilate spoke these words in mockery and sarcasm, but our Blessed Mother knew them to be true.

What a contrast was thus presented for all to see. On one side there was Pilate, the worldly governor who had authority to crucify Jesus or release Him. On the other side was Jesus, bound hand and foot, treated as a criminal and seated on the judgment seat. He was about to be condemned to death by an earthly ruler. But from a divine perspective, Jesus was about to be enthroned on the true Judgment Seat of Grace. He wore a crown of thorns, but from the perspective of Heaven it was a crown of glory. He was about to receive the sentence of death, but from the perspective of Heaven it was a sentence that set all sinners free.

As our Blessed Mother stood before the Cross of her Son, she would have pondered these words of Pilate over and over: "Behold, your king!" Mother Mary did this perfectly. She beheld Him with her eyes and adored Him with her heart. She acknowledged His kingship and pledged her total submission to His rule. He was not only her Son, He was also her King in every way. The grace and mercy flowing from His throne of the Cross directed every moment of her life.

Too often in life, we fall into the error of valuing earthly power more than Heavenly power. But the kingship of Jesus should teach us that earthly power pales in comparison to the Heavenly authority Jesus exercised. He allowed men to treat Him as a criminal. But He exercised an authority that far surpassed the temporal influence of these earthly "kings." Jesus' Kingdom was not of this world. It was in the order of grace and mercy. Our Blessed Mother knew and pondered this, and she chose her Son as her eternal King. "Behold, my Son, my King!" she would have prayed.

Reflect, today, upon which kingdom you participate in more fully. The kingdoms of this world need to be transformed by the one and only Kingdom of God. We must live in this world but not be a part of it. We must allow the dictates of the King of Grace and Mercy to rule our lives and we must not allow ourselves to become intoxicated with the temporal "power" that this world offers. Choose Jesus as your King as you stand beside His loving mother.

My dearest Mother, you understood well that the disingenuous words spoken by Pilate contained a much deeper truth than he understood. Your Son was King indeed. He was the King of Heaven and one day His Kingdom would transform even the visible world when every knee would bow before Him.

My dear Mother, pray for me that I may always keep my eyes upon the true Kingdom of Heaven and that I may never be drawn into the corruption of earthly power. Pray for me that I may be an instrument of the dictates of love pouring forth from the throne of your divine Son.

My dear Lord and King, I behold You and acknowledge You as the ruler of my life. May every breath I take, every word I speak and every action I perform be done at Your gentle command. I choose You, this day, as the sole and complete ruler of my life.

Mother Mary, pray for me. Jesus, I trust in You.

Day Twenty-Three – The Sentence of Death

> When Pilate saw that he was not succeeding at all, but
> that a riot was breaking out instead, he took water and
> washed his hands in the sight of the crowd, saying, "I
> am innocent of this man's blood. Look to it
> yourselves." And the whole people said in reply, "His
> blood be upon us and upon our children." Then he
> released Barabbas to them, but after he had Jesus
> scourged, he handed him over to be crucified.
> Matthew 27:24-26

The decision had been made. Pilate had declared that he
believed Jesus was innocent, but because of the hostility and
threats of the chief priests and the crowds, he ordered that
Jesus be crucified. This was the easiest thing for Pilate to do
to avoid an uprising. Pilate acted in a cowardly way and then
declared that he was innocent of Jesus' blood. The chief
priests, elders and all who were present cried out "His blood
be upon us and upon our children."

What did our Blessed Mother think as she heard Pilate
pronounce the sentence of death upon her Son? What did she
think when the religious leaders and agitators within the
crowds gave their strong vocal consent? Perhaps, as she
continued to ponder these words, "His blood be upon us and
upon our children," she would have transformed that
statement into her deepest prayer.

As she stood before her Son on the Cross and contemplated
these words spoken just hours before, our Blessed Mother
would have realized they expressed Jesus' deepest desire. He
desired that His Precious Blood would indeed be poured out
upon all people, including those responsible for His death. He
would have desired that His Precious Blood would cover them
all, washing away their sins and sanctifying them so that they

could enter His eternal Kingdom. Mother Mary would have shared this same desire of our Lord. She would have forgiven the cowardice of Pilate and the harshness of the crowds.

We are all called to shed our blood for the sanctification of others. Though Jesus is the one and only Savior of the World, we are called to participate in His offering. We are called to unite our own daily sacrifices with His one eternal sacrifice. To do this, we must let go of every bit of our wounded pride, anger, hurt and vengeance. We must desire that our own daily sacrifice be offered for the good of all, including those who have sinned against us. We must turn away from a desire for earthly justice and realize that mercy and forgiveness bring forth the perfection of God's justice.

Reflect, today, upon our Blessed Mother as she contemplated these words of the people, "His blood be upon us and upon our children." Know that this became her deepest prayer during Jesus' three hours on the Cross. As you contemplate Mother Mary praying these words, try to unite your own mistreatment, suffering and hurt to the Cross of Christ. Know that the free embrace of your own sacrifice can be turned into a blanket of grace and mercy for those who need it the most.

My dear Mother, through the ponderings of your Immaculate Heart, you were able to transform the harsh words of your Son's persecutors into your own beautiful prayer. You were able to see that the blood shed by your Son was the source of grace and mercy needed, if not sought, by all.

My loving Mother, pray for me that I may imitate your merciful heart and pray that your Son's blood be poured out in abundance upon all those in need.

My suffering Lord, give me the grace to unite my own sufferings with Yours and to unite the injustices I endure with the injustice of the shedding of Your Precious Blood. Help me to see all things through Your eyes and to love all people with Your Sacred Heart.

My dear Mother, pray for me. Jesus, I trust in You.

Day Twenty-Four – The Gaze of Mother and Son

Consider how the Son met His Mother on His way to Calvary. Jesus and Mary gazed at each other and their looks became as so many arrows to wound those hearts which loved each other so tenderly.

My most loving Jesus, by the pain You suffered in this meeting grant me the grace of being truly devoted to Your most holy Mother. And You, my Queen, who was overwhelmed with sorrow, obtain for me by Your prayers a tender and a lasting remembrance of the passion of Your divine Son. I love You, Jesus, my Love, above all things. I repent of ever having offended You. Never allow me to offend You again. Grant that I may love You always; and then do with me as You will. (Fourth Station of the Cross, by Saint Alphonsus Liguori)

How could Mother Mary ever forget this moment when she met her Son on His way to Calvary? As she stood before the Cross of her Son, she would have replayed this holy meeting over and over again in her mind and heart. As Jesus was carrying His Cross to Calvary, they lived this most tender moment as if they were one.

After falling for the first time, He got up and continued His journey. Through all the pain and blood, He received the momentary consolation of a gaze of love from His mother. Their eyes met and their hearts united in sorrow and in joy.

Sorrow filled their Sacred and Immaculate Hearts as they felt the deep pain of the other. Jesus, looking at His dear mother, was immediately aware of the sword that pierced her Immaculate Heart as she watched Him so cruelly treated. Our Blessed Mother looked at Jesus and saw not only the Savior of the World, she also saw her own child whom she loved with all her heart.

Joy and sorrow co-mingled in their hearts as they each sensed and experienced the powerful emotions of their mother-child bond. Love was more powerful than suffering, and salvation was more powerful than death. The interior joy they felt, knowing that Jesus was bringing forth the greatest grace the world had ever known, filled mother and Son in this moment and gave them both the strength they needed to bring this sacrifice to completion.

Each one of us has the opportunity in life to ease the suffering of another by our tender care and gaze of love. When we encounter another in need, we have the opportunity to express our compassion. While pity looks down on another from a perspective of superiority, true compassion suffers with another with authentic empathy. True compassion shoulders another's cross, enters into another's mind and heart, and walks arm and arm with another down every rough road.

Reflect, today, upon this beautiful but sorrowful scene of the gaze of love shared by mother and Son on the way to Calvary. Reflect also on the fact that both mother and Son meet you on your own journey toward the Cross. No matter what you encounter, no matter what you endure, they are there, attentive to you, loving you and offering their hearts to you. Seek also to emulate the hearts of Jesus and our Blessed Mother to those whom you encounter each day. Grow in compassion and concern for all who suffer, being present to them as they go step by step on their personal *via dolorosa* (sorrowful way).

My Sorrowful Mother, you already endured so much. But you would not miss this short moment in which you could express your tender love for your Son. As you looked at Him, your heart intertwined with His. You felt the pain He felt. You communicated a supernatural joy that strengthened His resolve to give His life for the Salvation of the world.

My dear Mother, pray for me that I may be open to your motherly concern for my life. As I carry my cross and endure the sufferings that befall me, intercede for me and open my soul to the strength of your Son as it flows through your own tender heart.

My suffering Lord, as You continued on Your journey to Calvary after falling for the first time, You looked at Your mother with such love. Your concern was not for Yourself, it was for Your mother and for all who would receive the grace of Your Cross. May I be one of those, dear Lord, who opens my heart to You at all times and who absorbs the graces You offer so that I can follow in Your footsteps.

Mother of Mercy, pray for me. Jesus, I trust in You.

Day Twenty-Five – Jesus Falls

> "Come to me, all you who labor and are burdened, and I will give you rest. Take my yoke upon you and learn from me, for I am meek and humble of heart; and you will find rest for yourselves. For my yoke is easy, and my burden light." Matthew 11:28-30

Jesus, under the weight of the Cross, fell to the ground. Simon, a foreigner, was pressed into service to help Jesus carry His Cross. But even with the help of Simon, Jesus falls again and again.

As our Blessed Mother watched in sorrow as her Son fell to the ground three times, physically exhausted and barely able to go on, she may have recalled Jesus' own words early on in His public ministry: "Come to me, all you who labor and are burdened, and I will give you rest." How deeply she must have felt these words resounding in her Immaculate Heart. "My Son, my dear Son, come to me, come to my heart and rest."

And though she could not physically help her Son carry His Cross, she would have been filled with much gratitude as she saw Simon the Cyrene pressed into service by the guards to help Jesus carry on. Though Simon helped reluctantly, his help was a shining witness. Through Simon, our Blessed Mother knew that the prayer of her heart was answered. She knew that the Father in Heaven was helping Jesus carry the weight of the Cross with the assistance of this foreigner.

As Mother Mary stood before the Cross of Jesus and recalled the assistance of Simon, she would have known that he set forth a powerful example for all people. She would have pondered the act of Simon as a symbol for all Christians. We all are called to help carry the Cross of Christ. No one is exempt from the Cross. Jesus Himself promised the Cross to us when He said, "Whoever wishes to come after me must deny himself, take up his cross, and follow me" (Matthew 16:24). The Cross is not an option, it's a reality, especially the cross of death itself.

The real question for everyone is whether we will embrace the Cross willingly or begrudgingly. Our Blessed Mother desired to lift the heavy burden of the Cross with all her heart. And though Simon did so hesitantly, he made the choice and served in time of need.

Reflect, today, upon the heavy burdens that others carry in life. When you see them and are made aware of their struggles, what is your reaction? Do you turn from them and run from their struggle? Or do you turn towards them, fully embracing the cross they carry. Seek to imitate Simon's act of carrying the Cross. Seek to imitate our Blessed Mother's burning desire to do the same with perfect love. Do so without hesitation and you will discover the sweetness of the Cross of Christ as you alleviate another's burden.

My dearest Mother, as you watched Simon be pressed into service to help your Son carry His Cross, your heart was filled with gratitude. Your prayer was answered as the Father provided the physical strength needed by your Son to carry on. Simon became that strength and a symbol of service to others.

Dear Mother, please point me to those in my life who are in need. Help me to seek out those who carry heavy crosses and to willingly, joyfully and freely seek to help them. Lend me the hands of Simon and your own tender heart so that the burden of many may be lifted.

My exhausted Lord, there are times in life when I fall. Not because of the loss of physical strength, but because of my sin. Help me to be open to the help of others when I am in need. Help me, also, to have the wisdom and love I need to reach out to those who are heavily burdened.

Mother Mary, pray for me. Jesus, I trust in You.

Day Twenty-Six – The Holy Women and Veronica

A large crowd of people followed Jesus, including many women who mourned and lamented him. Jesus turned to them and said, "Daughters of Jerusalem, do not weep for me; weep instead for yourselves and for your children, for indeed, the days are coming when people will say, 'Blessed are the barren, the wombs that never bore and the breasts that never nursed.' At that time people will say to the mountains, 'Fall upon us!' and to the hills, 'Cover us!' for if these things are done when the wood is green what will happen when it is dry?" Luke 23:27-31

Many holy women followed Jesus to the mount of Golgotha, watching and weeping. Our Lord paused in His path toward Calvary and spoke to their hearts of the true horrors to come. He prophesied the evil that many would suffer and the sin into which many would fall. Jesus' death is painful, yes. But the greatest tragedies are yet to come when persecutions will burn so hot against believers that the resulting fire will be like one fueled by the driest timbers.

One of the holy women, Veronica, approached Jesus in silence. She removed a clean veil and carefully wiped His bloody face with it. This wordless act of love was received by Jesus with serenity. Posterity has reciprocated Veronica's small act of charity by forever blessing and honoring her holy name.

As our Blessed Mother stood before the Cross of her divine Son, she would have pondered the encounters these holy women had with her Son. She would have been filled with gratitude for the care and concern these women had shown to Jesus and she would have been touched by their compassionate tears.

But she would have also reflected on Jesus' words, "Daughters of Jerusalem, do not weep for me; weep instead for yourselves and for your children." Mother Mary would have indeed taken these words to heart. Though her heart was filled with a holy sorrow at the Crucifixion of her Son, her deepest sorrow was for those who would reject the gift her Son was offering them. She would have been keenly aware that Jesus' death was meant for all, but that not all would accept the grace that flowed from His perfect sacrifice.

Mother Mary was aware of the fact that these holy women, and their children, would later suffer for their love of Jesus. They would be invited to participate in His own Cross in a more powerful way than the holy women first did on that Friday in Jerusalem. As these women and their spiritual heirs began to receive the Eucharist after Jesus' Resurrection, and began to enter into a deep spiritual communion with Him through prayer, they would not only be filled with joy, they would also be compelled to carry the Cross of discipleship.

Reflect, today, upon one "consequence" of being a follower of Jesus. If you choose to follow Jesus, you will also be invited to share in His suffering and death so that you may share in His Resurrection. Allow your heart to be filled with the same compassion as these holy women. Direct that compassion to those caught in a life of sin. Weep for them. Pray for them. Love them. Weep also for those who suffer on account of Christ. Let your tears be ones of holy sorrow like the tears that rolled down the cheeks of our Blessed Mother and these holy women of Jerusalem.

My sorrowful Mother, you watched as these holy women wept at the suffering of your own Son. You saw the tears they shed and the compassion they felt. Pray for me that I may also have holy tears as I see the suffering of the innocent, and fill my heart with compassion and concern.

Loving Mother, pray also that I may have a heart of sorrow for those who live in sin. Your Son died for all, but many have not accepted His mercy.

Let my sorrow for sin be converted into tears of grace so that others may come to know your Son through me.

My merciful Lord, may I see Your agony and death as the glorious means of salvation for the world. Fill my heart with true sorrow for those who do not open themselves to Your love. May that sorrow become a means of grace and mercy for those who are most in need.

My dear Mother, pray for me. Jesus, I trust in You.

Day Twenty-Seven – Humiliation: Stripped of Garments

> When the soldiers had crucified Jesus, they took his clothes and divided them into four shares, a share for each soldier. They also took his tunic, but the tunic was seamless, woven in one piece from the top down. So they said to one another, "Let's not tear it, but cast lots for it to see whose it will be," in order that the passage of scripture might be fulfilled [that says]: "They divided my garments among them, and for my vesture they cast lots." This is what the soldiers did. John 19:23-24

What could be more humiliating than to be stripped of your garments before your own mother and friends and then to be hung upon a cross to die. But Jesus was stripped of His garments for a reason. Everything earthly had been freely sacrificed by Him and He died with nothing of His own in this world. His sacred flesh revealed the dignity of His sacred soul which was loved and adored by His dear mother.

As our Blessed Mother stood before the Cross gazing at her Son after they had stripped Him of His garments, she would have been reminded of the day of His birth when He came into the world with nothing. And she may have recalled the words from Scripture spoken by Job, "Naked I came forth from my mother's womb, and naked shall I go back there. The LORD gave and the LORD has taken away; blessed be the name of the LORD!" (Job 1:21) Our Blessed Mother witnessed the very beginning of Jesus' earthly life and now was witnessing the very end.

The stripping of our Lord's garments revealed that the sacredness of His life was not in what He obtained or had as a possession; rather, the sacredness and value of His life was solely about who He was. He was God in the flesh, God incarnate, the Second Person of the Most Holy Trinity in bodily form. In His flesh was the unity of God and man and our Blessed Mother was privileged to witness this reality of the Incarnation one last time as Jesus hung upon the Cross. She gazed at Him and beheld God in the flesh.

In our own lives we must strive to see the value of who we are. Too often, we fall into the trap of taking our identity and value in the things of this world. Many can erroneously think, "If I accomplish much in the eyes of the world then I have value." Or, "The more possessions I have the greater my happiness will be."

We must strive to learn a lesson from the stripped body of our blessed Savior as He hung upon the Cross before His mother and before the world. Just like Jesus, our dignity comes from our union with God. We have value and worth not as a result of what we accomplish or obtain in this life. Rather, we have dignity because we have allowed the God of Heaven to come to Earth and enter into our own flesh and blood. Our dignity is on account of the continuation of the Incarnation of God alive in our lives.

Reflect, today, upon the most sacred image adored by our Blessed Mother. Join her in adoring the sacred dignity of her Son, the Son of God and the Son of Man. Recognize that Jesus' Incarnation also raised you to the heights of Heaven and strive to see the presence of the Son of God alive in your own life.

My dearest Mother, you stood before the Cross of your Son adoring His bruised and beaten body. This was the same body that had come forth into the world from your own sacred womb. Now this Child of yours was once again stripped bare in your sight. But as you gazed at Him, once again, you saw what you had seen every day of His life. You saw God in the flesh.

My dear Mother, pray for me that I may always see the dignity of others not on account of what they have or what they accomplish, but on account of who they are. Help me to see all people as sons and daughters of our loving God in Heaven.

My precious Lord, I invite You, this day and always, to unite Yourself to me. Come live within me and make my heart and soul, my flesh and bones, a continuing presence of Your Incarnation. Help me to see the dignity I obtain in life by becoming one with You.

Mother Mary, pray for me. Jesus, I trust in You.

Day Twenty-Eight – His Hands and Feet

> Consider Jesus, thrown down upon the cross, He stretched out His arms and offered to His eternal Father the sacrifice of His life for our salvation. They nailed His hands and feet, and then, raising the cross, left Him to die in anguish. (Eleventh Station of the Cross, by Saint Alphonsus Liguori)

As our Blessed Mother stood before the Cross of her Son, she was compelled by love to adore the wounds in His sacred hands and feet. She was drawn to gaze at the nails that pierced her Son as they fixed His hands to the Cross. Such cruelty. So merciless. The pain caused by these nails was excruciating. All our Blessed Mother could do was to watch in love and ponder the wounds inflicted upon her divine Son.

Why did they nail Jesus to the Cross? It was to fulfill the Scripture that He was nailed to the Cross. Isaiah the prophet said, "But he was pierced for our sins, crushed for our iniquity. He bore the punishment that makes us whole, by his wounds we were healed" (Isaiah 53:5).

"By His wounds we were healed." What a mysterious statement. How is it that the wounds of Jesus bring healing to the world? As our Blessed Mother contemplated this great mystery, and adored the wounds in her Son's hands and feet, she would have recalled the rest of Isaiah's prophecy, "We had all gone astray like sheep, all following our own way; But the LORD laid upon him the guilt of us all. Though harshly treated, he submitted and did not open his mouth; Like a lamb led to slaughter or a sheep silent before shearers, he did not open his mouth" (Isaiah 53:6-7).

Jesus embraced the Cross and willingly allowed Himself to be pierced for our transgressions. He took upon Himself the consequences of our sin and paid the price of death. In this act of freely giving His life as the spotless and innocent Lamb,

He destroyed the law of death and transformed sin and death into new life.

The mystery of Jesus' suffering as the innocent Lamb is deep and beyond comprehension. Our Blessed Mother contemplated this great mystery of suffering in her heart and knew, by faith, that every wound and every nail brought untold grace into the world. She saw in her crucified Son the effects of the sins of the world. But she also saw sin destroyed by His free and innocent embrace.

Very often we fail to understand that our Lord's suffering and death is a mystery. We fail to comprehend and to be grateful for the great mystery of His innocent suffering which sets us free.

Reflect, today, upon the wounds of the innocent Lamb of God. Gaze at His wounds with our Blessed Mother. See His wounds as the price of your sins. Allow your heart to be filled with deep gratitude as you ponder this unfathomable mystery.

My dear Mother, only your faith could penetrate the mystery of suffering, just as the nails penetrated the hands and feet of your divine Son. Only your love could comprehend the mercy and healing offered by your Son's wounds. Draw me into this gaze of yours so that my mind and heart may penetrate its meaning.

My dear Mother, I also offer to you and to your Son the wounds that afflict me unjustly. May I never complain or turn away from the opportunity to give myself freely, and to accept suffering, for the healing of others. Teach me to imitate this great mystery of your Son in my own life.

My pierced Jesus, Your mother gazed with love at the wounds in Your hands and feet. She saw and believed in the healing that was made possible by Your free embrace of such cruelty. Give me the grace I need to also gaze at Your sacred wounds and to penetrate the meaning of their mystery. I thank You, dear Lord, for the abundant mercy You have poured forth from Your sacred wounds.

Mother Mary, pray for me. Jesus, I trust in You.

Day Twenty-Nine – Jesus is Lifted Up on the Cross

> "Now is the time of judgment on this world; now the ruler of this world will be driven out. And when I am lifted up from the earth, I will draw everyone to myself." He said this indicating the kind of death he would die. John 12:31-32

Jesus' prophecy was fulfilled. He was lifted up on the Cross for all to see. Among those seeing this horrific sight was His own dear mother.

Mother Mary heard this prophecy spoken by Jesus during His public ministry. She pondered His words over the years just as she had pondered the words spoken by Simeon when she and Saint Joseph presented Jesus in the temple, "And you yourself a sword will pierce so that the thoughts of many hearts may be revealed" (Luke 2:35).

Mother Mary's Immaculate Heart was now fully pierced as she gazed at her Son, lifted up on the Cross for all to see. And though this sight caused deep sorrow and pain, our Blessed Mother saw the blessing of her Son being lifted up as she pondered His own words. "Now the ruler of this world will be driven out. And when I am lifted up from the earth, I will draw everyone to myself."

Though painful to see, our Blessed Mother knew that her Son's Crucifixion was accomplishing the greatest good ever known. She knew that He had suddenly destroyed the "ruler of this world" and had driven him out from the hearts of those who turned to the Cross. She knew that her Son's Cross would draw many to Heaven and free them from eternal death. Mother Mary herself was the first to be drawn to her Son's Cross and to be bathed in the grace of His unending mercy.

Have you allowed the power of the Cross to transform your own life? Have you joined our Blessed Mother as she stood before the Cross with her eyes fixed in love at the image of her salvation? Have you allowed the power of the Cross to drive out the ruler of this world from your own heart? Have you allowed Jesus' Cross to draw you to Himself and to the Father?

Reflect, today, upon these questions as you reflect upon your Lord being lifted up upon the Holy Cross. See Him hanging there and know that this is the image of your own salvation. Allow yourself to be drawn to Him and allow His Precious Blood to cover you, driving the evil one and all sin from your life. Reflect, ponder, be open and receive. The Lord was lifted up for you. Allow the power of the Cross to change your life.

My dearest Mother, though you gazed at the horrific sight of your Son's brutal Crucifixion, you remembered the words He spoke in which He revealed the power of His sacrifice. You were aware of the deep truth that His Cross was destroying the evil one and all sin, and that all who gazed upon your Son in faith with you would be drawn to the glory of Heaven.

Pray for me, dear Mother, that I may be one of those who stand with you in the shadow of the Cross. Help me to be strengthened by your witness. Point me always to your Son so that I may receive the abundance of grace poured out on Calvary.

My crucified Lord, I thank You for the unfathomable gift of the Cross. Draw me in, dear Lord, and sanctify me by Your perfect sacrifice of love. Heal me, renew me, give me new life and drive all sin from my life. I thank You Lord for all You have done and open my heart to all that You still wish to do in me.

Mother Mary, pray for me. Jesus, I trust in You.

Day Thirty – "Father, Forgive Them, For They Know Not What They Do"

> When they came to the place called the Skull, they crucified him and the criminals there, one on his right, the other on his left. [Then Jesus said, "Father, forgive them, they know not what they do."] Luke 23:33-34a

As our Blessed Mother stood before the Cross of her Son, she heard Him speak these words with compassion, conviction and mercy, "Father, forgive them, they know not what they do." What would Mother Mary have thought as she heard her Son speak these words about those who were responsible for His brutal torture and death? What would she, as a mother, think about this prayer of her Son?

These are the first of seven statements of our divine Lord spoken from the Cross. In many ways, they are foundational teachings for the entire Christian life. These words about forgiveness are integral to that foundation.

As our Blessed Mother heard these words of her Son, she would have immediately echoed these sentiments spoken from the heart of her Son. As Jesus cried out to the Father, begging for mercy upon those responsible for His brutal Crucifixion, so our Blessed Mother would have cried out as in one song of mercy and praise. Their hearts of mercy were united. One unwavering song of forgiveness was sung by two voices, He who suffered physically and she who suffered silently.

To forgive without reserve in such a moment is almost beyond human comprehension. It's beyond what our fallen human nature can immediately grasp. So often we want revenge and worldly justice. We want others to be held accountable and judged for their wrongs. But this is not our role. The Father in Heaven is the only judge. We have only the duty to forgive. And we must do so over and over again.

Who has hurt you? Against whom do you hold a grudge? Whom have you failed to forgive? Forgiving another does not excuse their sin. On the contrary, an act of forgiveness acknowledges sin as a prior act in need of mercy. Forgiveness offers mercy even when it is not asked for or even deserved. Mercy must be given by us without reserve and in every situation in life on account of the unlimited mercy given to us by God. Mercy flows downhill.

Reflect, today, upon the Mother of God seeing with her own eyes the most brutal treatment of her Son. As you ponder her at the foot of the Cross, listen to Jesus speak those powerful words, "Father, forgive them, for they know not what they do." Listen to those words with our Blessed Mother and know that she spoke them with her Son without reserve. Join in their prayer and offer it for those whom you need to forgive.

My dearest Mother of Mercy, you listened in love to your Son speak these most incredible words, "Father, forgive them, for they know not what they do." These words were like an arrow of mercy piercing your heart. And you responded to these words with your own prayer of mercy for all those who had sinned against your Son.

My dear Mother, pray for me that I may imitate this prayer of forgiveness in my own life. Pray for me that I may not hesitate in offering this mercy to all who have sinned against me.

My Merciful Lord, You did not hesitate to forgive those who gravely sinned against You. They treated You with cruelty beyond comprehension, yet You forgave them with perfect mercy. Give me the grace I need, dear Lord, to forgive those who have sinned against me. Replace anger and hate with love and mercy.

Mother Mary, pray for me. Jesus, I trust in You.

Day Thirty-One – "Today You Will be With Me in Paradise"

> Now one of the criminals hanging there reviled Jesus, saying, "Are you not the Messiah? Save yourself and us." The other, however, rebuking him, said in reply, "Have you no fear of God, for you are subject to the same condemnation? And indeed, we have been condemned justly, for the sentence we received corresponds to our crimes, but this man has done nothing criminal." Then he said, "Jesus, remember me when you come into your kingdom." He replied to him, "Amen, I say to you, today you will be with me in Paradise." Luke 23:39-43

What a powerful exchange this was between Jesus and the two criminals who were crucified with Him on His right and on His left. Our Blessed Mother stood in silence, listening to them converse. There is no doubt that as she heard the words of her Son, her heart leaped for joy.

This is a powerful scene. The two criminals represent all of us, either on Jesus' right or on His left. Each one of us speaks to Jesus in similar words. Each one of us will either receive the silence of our Lord or hear Him say, "Today you will be with me in Paradise."

Which criminal represents you more accurately? One criminal is filled with self-righteousness stemming from pride. The other is filled with sorrow stemming from humility. Both are guilty but only one is forgiven. They both acknowledge Jesus as the Messiah but only one takes ownership of his sin.

The first criminal speaks, "Save yourself and us." What he fails to see is that Jesus is in the very process of doing just that. By suffering and dying He is destroying sin and winning salvation for all who humbly seek His mercy. His death is the gateway to Paradise. The first criminal fails to see this.

Instead, he seeks immediate earthly "salvation" by challenging Jesus to save him from death on the cross.

But the other criminal identifies the glorious mission of our Lord. He acknowledges that his own death is an act of justice due to his sins. "We have been condemned justly," he professes. But the "good thief" does not stop there. He humbly asks Jesus to remember him as Jesus enters into His Kingdom. Jesus assents and offers this criminal the grace won by Jesus' own imminent death and promises him Paradise.

As our Blessed Mother looked on, her heart was filled with both joy and sorrow. Her sorrow was on account of the first criminal who failed to humbly acknowledge his guilt. Her joy was on account of the other criminal who humbled himself before her Son and received eternal life. Mother Mary saw, as her Son hung on the Cross, the promise of Paradise being petitioned for and then granted. The joy she felt by witnessing the salvation of this criminal consoled the sorrow she felt at her Son's brutal treatment.

We are all called to bring joy to the heart of our Blessed Mother. We do so when we humbly admit that we, too, are "criminals" in the sense that we are sinners. The punishment we deserve is death. But if we humbly admit this truth, we must also find the courage to beg our Lord for His mercy and to welcome us into Paradise.

Reflect, today, upon the words of this good thief. "Jesus, remember me when you come into your kingdom." Our Lord died in order to pry open the gates of Paradise first shut by Adam's sin. Reflect, also, upon the joy you bring to our Blessed Mother every time you humble yourself before the grace won by the Cross of her Son.

Dearest Mother, as you stood before your Son and heard Him promise salvation to the thief who repented, your heart leaped with pure joy. I pray that I may also bring joy to your heart as you see the grace of the Cross of your Son pour down upon me.

My dear Mother, pray for me that I may also take joy in the repentance of all sinners. Too often I find myself judgmental and slow to forgive. May my heart imitate your pure love and may I find joy in the conversion of all who turn to your Son.

My forgiving Savior, I am condemned justly for my sins and deserve death. Forgive me and have mercy on me, dear Lord. I repent of my sins and ask You for the grace to be remembered by You in Your glorious Kingdom.

Mother Mary, pray for me. Jesus, I trust in You.

Day Thirty-Two – "Woman, Behold Your Son...Behold Your Mother"

> Standing by the cross of Jesus were his mother and his mother's sister, Mary the wife of Clopas, and Mary of Magdala. When Jesus saw his mother and the disciple there whom he loved, he said to his mother, "Woman, behold, your son." Then he said to the disciple, "Behold, your mother." And from that hour the disciple took her into his home. John 19:25-27

What a beautiful act of love offered by the Son of Mary as He prepared to breathe His last. His concern was not for Himself. He was not wrought in self-pity and despair. Rather, He was concerned about those whom He loved. First, He reached out to the thief on the cross promising him Paradise. And then He entrusted His own dear mother to His beloved disciple John. "Woman, behold, your son." "Behold, your mother."

For this precious moment, the Mother of God took her eyes off her Son Jesus to gaze with love upon John, her new child in grace. John, the one disciple who had remained close to Jesus throughout His suffering and death, and who remained with our Blessed Mother as she stood before the Cross, turned and gazed with love upon his new mother in grace.

This act of giving and receiving was not meant only for our Blessed Mother and for John. It was meant as a command for us all. We are all invited to be present before the foot of the Cross in the person of this beloved disciple. Jesus looks at all of us from the Cross and says, "Behold, your mother." And He directs His own dear mother to turn to each one of us with love and affection, seeing her own precious child in each one of us.

Our Blessed Mother is the new Eve, the new Mother of All the Living in the divine order of grace. She is the Mother and Queen of the new Kingdom and the new Family of God. If we wish to be members of that new Kingdom of Grace, we must lovingly accept our new mother.

John took our Blessed Mother into his own home, loving her and being loved by her. Mother Mary's maternal care for John enabled him to embrace the will of God until the end of his life. We, too, must take our Blessed Mother into the home of our hearts and embrace her as our own. She, in turn, will embrace us and point us to her divine Son.

Reflect, today, upon these beautiful words of Jesus. Hear them spoken to you. Hear Jesus say to you, "Behold your mother." Behold the Blessed Virgin Mary, the Mother of God and the Queen of Heaven and Earth. Turn to her, love her and receive her motherly guidance and care. Allow her to embrace you and to welcome you into her heart.

My dearest Mother and Queen, as you stood before the Cross of your Son, the one thing that drew your eyes from your Son was the invitation from Jesus to behold your new child in grace. I am that child, dear Mother, and I thank you for the gaze of love you bestow upon me.

My dear Mother, I accept you into the home of my heart to be my spiritual mother in the order of grace. I accept you as my queen and seek your maternal care and guidance. Draw me to your divine Son, dear Mother, and pray for me that I may seek Him above all else in life.

My loving Lord Jesus, as You hung upon the Cross, Your deepest desire was the salvation of souls. From Your Cross, You look down upon me, a lowly sinner, and entrust Your own mother to me. I thank You for this unfathomable gift and I accept the maternal care of the Queen of the Universe and the Mother of All.

Mother Mary, pray for me. Jesus, I trust in You.

Day Thirty-Three – "My God, My God, Why Have You Forsaken Me?"

> From noon onward, darkness came over the whole land until three in the afternoon. And about three o'clock Jesus cried out in a loud voice, "Eli, Eli, lema sabachthani?" which means, "My God, my God, why have you forsaken me?" Matthew 27:45-46

These words of Jesus must have pierced the heart of our Blessed Mother deeply. She stood close to Him, gazing at Him with love, adoring His wounded body given for the world, and she heard this cry coming forth from the depths of His being.

"My God, my God..." He begins. As our Blessed Mother listened to her Son speak to His Father in Heaven, she would have found great consolation in her knowledge of His intimate relationship with the Father. She knew, better than anyone else, that Jesus and the Father were one. She had heard Him speak this way in His public ministry many times and she also knew by her motherly intuition and faith that her Son was the Son of the Father. And before her eyes Jesus was calling out to Him.

But Jesus went on asking, "...why have you abandoned me?" The sting to her heart would have been immediate as she sensed the interior suffering of her Son. She knew He was experiencing far more pain than any bodily wound could inflict. She knew He was experiencing a profound interior darkness. His words spoken from the Cross confirmed every motherly concern that she had.

As our Blessed Mother pondered these words of her Son, over and over in her heart, she would have come to understand that Jesus' interior suffering, His experience of isolation and spiritual loss of the Father, was a gift to the world. Her perfect faith would have led her to understand that Jesus was entering into the experience of sin itself. Though perfect and sinless in every way, He was allowing Himself to be drawn into the human experience that results from sin: separation from the Father. Though Jesus was never separated from the Father, He entered into the human experience of this separation so as to restore fallen humanity to the Father of Mercies in Heaven.

As we ponder this cry of pain coming forth from our Lord, we must all seek to experience it as our own. Our cry, unlike our Lord's, is a result of our sins. When we sin, we turn in on ourselves and enter into isolation and despair. Jesus came to destroy these effects and to restore us to the Father in Heaven.

Reflect, today, upon the profound love our Lord had for all of us in that He was willing to experience the consequences of our sins. Our Blessed Mother, as the most perfect mother, was with her Son every step of the way, sharing His pain and interior sufferings. She felt what He felt and it was her love, more than anything else, that expressed, and stood in for, the steadfast and unwavering presence of the Father in Heaven. The Father's love was made manifest through her heart as she gazed with love at her suffering Son.

My most loving Mother, your heart was pierced with pain as you shared in your Son's interior suffering. His cry of abandonment was one that expressed His perfect love. His words revealed that He was entering into the effects of sin itself and allowing His human nature to experience it and redeem it.

Dear Mother, stand by me as I go through life and feel the effects of my own sin. Though your Son was perfect, I am not. My sin leaves me isolated and sorrowful. May your motherly presence in my life always remind me that the Father never leaves me and is always inviting me to turn to His merciful Heart.

My abandoned Lord, You entered into the greatest agony any human could enter. You allowed Yourself to experience the effects of my own sin.

Give me the grace of turning to Your Father every time I sin so that I may merit the adoption won for me by Your Cross.

Mother Mary, pray for me. Jesus, I trust in You.

Day Thirty-Four – "I Thirst"

> After this, aware that everything was now finished, in order that the scripture might be fulfilled, Jesus said, "I thirst." There was a vessel filled with common wine. So they put a sponge soaked in wine on a sprig of hyssop and put it up to his mouth. John 19:28-29

As our Blessed Mother heard her Son speak these words, "I thirst," she would have immediately desired to satiate His thirst. She was attentive to His bodily thirst, but she was even more attentive to His spiritual thirst.

As the soldier took a sponge, soaked it in wine and placed it to His mouth, she would have received some consolation from this act of kindness. But she would have also seen great meaning in this act. The soldier was a symbol of fallen humanity and the sour wine was a symbol of our disordered state. But it was precisely our disordered state that Jesus longed to redeem. He did not desire "fresh wine" or "pure spring water." He desired fallen humanity. He thirsted for us to come to Him in our weakness and sin. Our Blessed Mother would have perceived this powerful symbolism.

Jesus still cries out today, "I thirst!" He thirsts for you. Too often we feel that we can only come to Him, to satiate His thirst, if we come in an angelic way. Too often we believe that Jesus only smiles at us when we come without sin. But this is not true. The reason that He died such a cruel death was so that we could come to Him in our own brokenness. We come to the suffering and thirsty Christ with our sin and disorder. We are not fresh wine, we are sour wine. But when we allow ourselves to come to our Lord in this state, His thirst is quenched.

What is the condition of your soul? Are you embarrassed by your sin? Do you adopt a false persona presuming that Jesus will only accept you if you are perfect? Nothing is further from the truth. Do not hesitate to come to our Lord with all your weaknesses, struggles and sins. Do not worry about what He will think or say. Come to Him. If you trust Him, your humble act of offering Him your sinful self will refresh His soul.

Reflect, today, upon those two sacred words of our dying Lord, "I thirst." Know that His thirst is for you and that He desires you just as you are. Go to Him, surrender to Him and delight Him. Our Blessed Mother is watching and waiting for you to satiate the longing within the Heart of her divine Son.

My dearest Mother, you were attentive to the spiritual thirst in the Heart of your Son. You were also attentive to the fact that His thirst was for me and for all humanity. Pray for me that I may be like that sour wine, lifted to the lips of your divine Son.

My loving Mother, pray for me that I may see my sin and may not hesitate to go to your Son in this state. I pray that I may have the courage I need to come in my weakness so as to satiate the Heart of your Son and your own Immaculate Heart.

My thirsting Lord, I know that Your words, spoken from the Cross, were words inviting me to satiate Your spiritual longing. Help me to trust that You love me as I am. Give me the courage I need to trust in Your mercy and to turn to You this day. I love You, dear Lord. Help me to love You more.

Mother Mary, pray for me. Jesus, I trust in You.

Day Thirty-Five – "It is Finished"

> When Jesus had taken the wine, he said, "It is finished." And bowing his head, he handed over the spirit. John 19:30

These words are of great relief to Jesus, His dear mother, and hopefully to all of us. "It is finished." Jesus' suffering had come to an end. His "thirst" was quenched by sour wine, a symbol of fallen humanity entering His very body. He had entered into all suffering, both interiorly and exteriorly, and now He was ready to enter into death itself. He spoke His final words and handed over His spirit to the Father.

As our Blessed Mother looked on, heard her Son speak His final words, and breathe His last, she would have felt a sense of relief. Jesus' long mission of salvation had been accomplished. Death was destroyed and now she only had to wait for His Resurrection.

Our Blessed Mother knew this was not the end. She knew that her Son would rise. He had taught many times "that the Son of Man must suffer greatly and be rejected by the elders, the chief priests, and the scribes, and be killed, and rise after three days" (Mark 8:31). Though the Apostles and other disciples did not understand this teaching, our Blessed Mother did. She witnessed His rejection, His death, and now turned her eyes toward His promised Resurrection.

This passage also states that Jesus "handed over His spirit." His life was not taken from Him. His death was a free choice by which He gave Himself over to death. He chose to enter into the ultimate effect of sin, death itself, so as to redeem death and make it the door to eternal life. The destruction of death was accomplished by God, the source of life, subsuming it into Himself. God wanted to come close to us by becoming man. He came so close to us that He allowed man to do Him violence. But the last chapter of Christ's life was yet to be written. His entrance into new life was about to begin.

These words of Jesus must take on great significance in our own lives. We must see ourselves standing by the Cross with our Blessed Mother and hear Jesus speak these words to us, personally. We must allow our Lord to look into our souls and say to us, "It is finished." Jesus speaks these words to each one of us. He says, "Your salvation is accomplished. My death has destroyed your own eternal death. My final word of victory has been spoken." As we ponder this sacred scene and hear these final words, we must seek to allow them to transform our very lives.

Reflect, today, upon whether you are attentive to these words of our Lord in your own life. Do you allow Him to apply His saving Sacrifice to your sins? Have you internalized this statement of promise from our Lord? Have you allowed the finality of His death to unite with your own sin? Reflect upon these three little words, this day, and allow the handing over of our Lord's Spirit to take hold of you and transform your life.

My dearest Mother, as you gazed intently at your Son, you heard Him announce that He had accomplished His mission. It was finished. He was faithful to the end. And though your heart was filled with sorrow as He died before your eyes, your spirit once again rejoiced as you witnessed the gift of salvation being accomplished for all humanity.

My loving Mother, pray for me that I may listen attentively to your Son as He speaks these sacred words. May I hear Him say to me, "It is finished! I have destroyed the effect of your sin. Death is no more."

My saving Lord, from the Cross You announced the fulfillment of Your divine mission. You proclaimed that You had destroyed death itself by the free offering of Your life. Help me to listen to You speak these words to my heart and to be open to the unfathomable gift of new life accomplished by Your willing Sacrifice.

Mother Mary, pray for me. Jesus, I trust in You.

Day Thirty-Six – "Father, Into Your Hands I Commend My Spirit"

> Jesus cried out in a loud voice, "Father, into your hands I commend my spirit"; and when he had said this he breathed his last. Luke 23:46

This perfect prayer, uttered from the depths of the Heart of our Lord, goes to the heart of life itself. It says it all. It's a prayer of complete surrender to the Father, a prayer of total abandonment and unwavering trust.

As our Blessed Mother stood at the foot of the Cross, there is no doubt that she joined her Son in His prayer of perfect surrender. She would have not only offered her own life once again to the Father, she would have also offered her Son.

Commending ourselves to the Father, in total abandonment, must become our daily mission. There is nothing in life more important than this. Jesus chose to make this prayer of surrender the last thing He spoke from the Cross as it is recorded by Saint Luke. Saint John's Gospel reveals Jesus saying, "It is finished." These two statements from our Lord make it clear that Jesus was perfectly one with the Father in His final moments on the Cross.

Think about that. As Jesus hung on the Cross, humiliated and in excruciating pain, He gave us a glorious example of surrender. Being perfect in every way, He did not turn in on Himself and wallow in self-pity, anger or regret. The cruelty He had received from so many did not deter Him from the continual surrender of His life to the Father and to His holy will. Instead, Jesus chose this most miserable persecuted state to profess His unending union with His Father.

Very often in our own lives, when crosses come our way, we begin to lose trust and hope in the Father. We carefully examine our wounds and ponder the injustices we've suffered.

We allow hurt and sorrow to turn our eyes from God and instead we gaze at ourselves.

This prayer, spoken by our Lord, and echoed in the heart of our Blessed Mother, was spoken in part as a lesson to each one of us. First, it was prayed because it was the perfect expression of who Jesus was. But secondly, it was spoken for us to imitate.

How deep is your surrender to the Father in Heaven? How often do you pray this prayer? And when you pray it, how completely does this prayer become an action in your life? To surrender is to act. It is more than a decision, it's a continual act of our will that deepens our surrender until it is complete and total.

Reflect, today, upon this perfect prayer of our Lord. "Father, into Your hands I commend my spirit." Pray it over and over. If you can, get on your knees or lie prostrate before our Lord. Reflect, also, upon this prayer as it would have been uttered by our Blessed Mother from the depths of her own heart. She offered her life continually and joined her Son in this perfect and final offering to the Father. She did so as she stood gazing at her Son with a mother's love.

My dearest Mother, as you stood before your Son and heard Him utter these sacred words, you made them your own. You freely and wholeheartedly offered your divine Son to the Father. You also offered your own life, once again, in union with the Sacrifice of your Son.

My loving Mother, pray for me that I may make my own life a perfect offering to the Father in Heaven. Help me, by your prayers and example, to hold nothing back. I give all to you, dear Mother, so that you may offer me to the Father in union with the offering of your Son.

My dying Lord, I commend my life into Your hands. I surrender all to You so that my life may be offered to the Father in union with Your perfect Sacrifice. Take me, dear Lord, receive me and do with me as You will.

Mother Mary, pray for me. Jesus, I trust in You.

Day Thirty-Seven – The Earth is Shaken

> And behold, the veil of the sanctuary was torn in two
> from top to bottom. The earth quaked, rocks were
> split, tombs were opened, and the bodies of many
> saints who had fallen asleep were raised. And coming
> forth from their tombs after his resurrection, they
> entered the holy city and appeared to many. Matthew
> 27:51-53

It must have been an awe-inspiring scene. As Jesus breathed
His last breath, surrendered His spirit, and pronounced that it
was finished, the world was shaken. There was suddenly a
powerful earthquake causing the veil in the temple to be torn
in two. As this happened, many who had died in grace came
back to life appearing in physical form to many.

As our Blessed Mother gazed upon her dead Son, she would
have been shaken to her very core. As the Earth shook the
dead to life, our Blessed Mother would have been immediately
aware of the effect of her Son's perfect Sacrifice. It was truly
finished. Death was destroyed. The veil separating fallen
humanity from the Father was destroyed. Heaven and Earth
were now reunited and new life was immediately offered to
those holy souls who were resting in their tombs.

The veil in the temple was thick. It separated the Holy of
Holies from the rest of the sanctuary. Only once a year was
the high priest allowed to enter this holy place to offer an
expiatory sacrifice to God for the sins of the people. So why
was the veil torn? Because the entire world had now become
a sanctuary, a new Holy of Holies. Jesus was the one and
perfect Lamb of Sacrifice replacing the many animal sacrifices
offered in the temple. What was local now became universal.
Repetitive animal sacrifices offered by man to God became
one sacrifice of God for man. Thus did the meaning of the
temple migrate and find a home in the sanctuary of every

Catholic Church. The Holy of Holies became obsolete by becoming common.

The meaning of Jesus' Sacrifice being offered on Mount Calvary for all to see is also significant. Public executions were performed to undo the public harm the executed supposedly caused. But Christ's execution became an invitation for all to discover the new Holy of Holies. No longer was the high priest alone allowed to enter sacred space. Instead, all were invited to approach the Sacrifice of the Spotless Lamb. Even more, we are invited into the Holy of Holies in order to unite our own lives to that of the Lamb of God.

As our Blessed Mother stood before the Cross of her Son and watched Him die, she would have been the first to fully unite her whole being to the Lamb of Sacrifice. She would have accepted His invitation to enter into the new Holy of Holies with her Son to adore her Son. She would have allowed her Son, the Eternal High Priest, to unite her to His Cross and offer her to the Father.

Reflect, today, upon the glorious truth that the new Holy of Holies is all around you. Daily, you are invited to climb upon the Cross of the Lamb of God to offer your life to the Father. Such a perfect offering will be received gladly by God the Father. Like all holy souls, you are invited to rise from the tomb of your sin and proclaim the glory of God in deed and in word. Reflect upon this glorious scene and rejoice that you are invited into the new Holy of Holies.

My dearest Mother, you were the first to go behind the veil and share in the Sacrifice of your Son. As High Priest, He made the perfect atonement for all sin. Though you were sinless, you offered your life to the Father with your Son.

My loving Mother, pray for me that I may become one with the Sacrifice of your Son. Pray that I may go beyond the veil of my sin and allow your divine Son, the Great High Priest, to offer me to the Father in Heaven.

My glorious High Priest and Lamb of Sacrifice, I thank You for inviting me to gaze upon the sacrificial offering of Your life. Invite me, I pray, into Your glorious Sacrifice so that I may become an oblation of love offered with You to the Father.

Mother Mary, pray for me. Jesus, I trust in You.

Day Thirty-Eight – The Soldier's Lance

> So the soldiers came and broke the legs of the first and then of the other one who was crucified with Jesus. But when they came to Jesus and saw that he was already dead, they did not break his legs, but one soldier thrust his lance into his side, and immediately blood and water flowed out. John 19:32-34

As our Blessed Mother stood gazing at the body of her Son, and saw the soldiers break the legs of the criminals on His right and left, she may have wondered what they were going to do to Jesus. As she looked on, she saw one of the soldiers drive a spear into His heart. She certainly felt the sharp pain of that piercing as she saw the cruelty continue. But what happened next was a sign that God's mercy is abundant. Immediately, blood and water flowed forth from Jesus' wounded Heart. Upon seeing this, our Blessed Mother would have immediately pondered its meaning.

Why did blood and water gush forth from the wounded Heart of Jesus as He hung dead upon the Cross? The blood and water were symbols of the sacramental life of the Church. Even in death, as Jesus' body was yet again abused by a soldier, He transformed the abuse into grace. As His Heart was pierced, He opened the floodgates of Heaven and poured forth an abundance of sacramental mercy. The blood was the pouring forth of the grace of the Most Holy Eucharist and the water was the pouring forth of the grace of Baptism.

As our Blessed Mother looked on with love and deep sorrow, she may not have fully comprehended that this was the beginning of the sacramental life of the Church as we now understand it. She would have known, by faith, that she was witnessing the beginnings of the new life of grace won by her Son. She would have known that this final act of cruelty was being transformed before her very eyes and turned into abundant blessings from Heaven.

What does your faith reveal to you about the Sacraments? Do you understand that the Sacraments are channels of the abundant mercy of God? Do you realize that the victory over sin and death, accomplished by Jesus on the Cross, flows to you by these seven streams of mercy? Do you understand the connection between this piercing of Jesus' Heart on the Cross and the Church's sacramental life?

Reflect, today, upon the extraordinary grace of the Sacraments. As you ponder the blood and water gushing forth from Jesus' side with our Blessed Mother, try to see this act in its deepest reality. See the grace of Baptism, the Holy Eucharist, and all the Sacraments at the moment of their birth. Ponder this: you stand before the Cross of our Lord; you bathe in His mercy; you see the flow from His wounded Heart; you accept it all. Hearing, you came. Coming, you saw. Seeing, you touched. And touching, you believed. His wounded Heart poured forth the Sacraments and you are invited to partake of the feast of grace.

My dearest Mother Mary, as you stood, gazing with love at the dead body of your beloved Son, you saw the soldier open His Heart with a spear. Though this caused excruciating pain in your own heart, it also filled you with an abundance of hope. The hope that filled your heart came from the knowledge that this last act of cruelty toward your Son opened the grace of Heaven and poured forth an abundance of mercy.

My dear Mother, pray for me that I may continually open my own heart to the mercy poured forth from the Heart of your beloved Son. May I especially be open to the grace given in abundance through the Sacraments.

My merciful Jesus, even in death You were abused as Your Heart was pierced by the soldier's lance. I thank You for the miraculous transformation of that act into the font of sacramental life within Your Church. I pray that I may always immerse myself in the mercy that gushed forth from Your divine Heart. May every drop of blood and water that poured forth from Your Heart land in my own soul.

Mother Mary, pray for me. Jesus, I trust in You.

Day Thirty-Nine – The Pietà

> Consider how, after Our Lord had died, He was taken down from the cross by two of His disciples, Joseph and Nicodemus, and placed in the arms of His afflicted Mother. She received Him with unutterable tenderness and pressed Him close to her bosom. (Thirteenth Station of the Cross, by Saint Alphonsus Liguori)

Our Blessed Mother was no longer standing before the foot of the Cross, gazing at her Son. Instead, Jesus' body was laid in her arms and she held Him close to her Immaculate Heart.

Though this was a moment of profound sorrow at the death of Jesus, it was also a moment of profound intimacy. As our Blessed Mother held the body of her Son, she knew it was not the end. Though her heart was pierced deeply, she knew that her pain would turn into joy. She was relieved that His earthly suffering was over, but her relief began to turn into hope and anticipation as she pondered His death and future Resurrection.

As our Blessed Mother held her Son close, she would have reflected upon Jesus' words spoken so often in His public ministry: "The Son of Man is to be handed over to men, and they will kill him, and he will be raised on the third day" (Matthew 17:22-23). She was witnessing His words come true. She knew that just as His prophecy regarding His death came true, so also His prophecy regarding His Resurrection would come true. "On the third day," He said. Our Blessed Mother knew that her pain would soon be turned into joy as she began her vigil in anticipation of her Son's Resurrection.

In most of our lives, we will face events that tempt us to despair. These events may be small encounters in our relationships with others that leave us feeling hopeless, discouraged and disappointed. At other times, we may encounter grave and tragic events that seem to leave us in utter desperation. The meaning of the *Pietà*, our Blessed Mother cradling the dead body of her Son, can never be exhausted. It's an image of *hope* in the midst of seeming hopelessness. It's an image of *love* that conquers all fear. It's an image of *faith* in the perfect plan of God no matter what comes.

Reflect, today, upon this tender image of our Blessed Mother with the sacred body of her divine Son resting in her lap. Reflect upon her pain and sorrow. Ponder also her faith in the promise of her Son, her hope in the fulfillment of that promise, and her love which enabled her to press on through her own grief. There is much we can learn from our Blessed Mother. Her heart, in particular, was one that shone brightly with the perfection of every virtue. She is a pillar of grace and strength surrounded by suffering. She is an example for all.

My dearest Mother, I can only try to imagine the sorrow you felt as you held your Son close to your Immaculate Heart. But I know that your sorrow was also mixed with hope as you anticipated the fulfillment of His promise. In faith, you knew this grief was not the end.

My loving Mother, strengthen my hope in the transformation of all sin and suffering in my life. As I encounter the hardships of life, pray for me that I may never despair. May I follow your example of faith, hope and love always. Please hold me close to your Immaculate Heart and pray that I may share in the Resurrection of your divine Son.

My dear Jesus, all earthly wisdom could not understand the meaning of Your suffering and death. By Your complete annihilation, You conquered the ruler of this world and destroyed his power over my life. May I see in this image of Your dead body a promise of Your

Resurrection. As I encounter struggles in life, give me hope and trust that final victory is always found in You.

Mother Mary, pray for me. Jesus, I trust in You.

Day Forty – The Silence of the Tomb

> They took the body of Jesus and bound it with burial
> cloths along with the spices, according to the Jewish
> burial custom. Now in the place where he had been
> crucified there was a garden, and in the garden a new
> tomb, in which no one had yet been buried. So they
> laid Jesus there because of the Jewish preparation day;
> for the tomb was close by. John 19:40-42

From an earthly perspective, all was lost, all was over. Jesus'
life had come to an end. His body lay in the tomb, the stone
covered the entrance and His followers were scattered. Where
was our Blessed Mother through all of this?

Though Scripture does not reveal her physical location, we can
be certain that our Blessed Mother kept vigil from Good
Friday until Easter Sunday. She kept vigil, first and foremost,
in her heart. Throughout her life she continually pondered
the mystery of her Son. She pondered His conception, His
birth, the flight into Egypt, His childhood, and every moment
of His public ministry. Over the past week she had pondered
His suffering and His brutal death. But through all of this
pondering, her Immaculate Heart was alive with confidence
and perfect trust. Her mind perceived the wisdom of the
Father's plan and her heart gave it her full assent. She knew,
without any shadow of a doubt, that the will of the Father was
unfolding perfectly.

As our Blessed Mother prayerfully pondered the life and death
of her Son that Holy Saturday, her heart would have been
filled with a peaceful excitement and joy. She may not have
known exactly how His Resurrection would unfold, but she
knew with conviction that He would soon return to her. She
did not allow despair to enter her Immaculate Heart for even
a moment. Instead, she kept a prayerful vigil for her Son and

awaited the fulfillment of His promise that He would rise on the third day. She had heard Him say this and she knew it was true. Her only duty now was to wait in vigilant prayer and expectation.

Hope is a supernatural gift from God. It's not just wishful thinking or optimism. Hope is a gift by which God makes an interior promise to each one of us. The promises He makes are the perfect revelation of His divine will. As we hear Him speak His promises, we must respond with faith.

Reflect, today, upon this most sacred scene of Holy Saturday. While many were filled with despair and confusion, our Blessed Mother continued her vigil of hope. She knew, without any doubt, that glorious things were still to come. She knew that her Son had completed His mission of salvation and was on the verge of restoring new life to all who would turn to Him in their need. Reflect upon your own hope in the promise of God in your life. Allow the example of our Blessed Mother to inspire you. Allow her prayers to transform you. Do not doubt for a moment that God has great things in mind for you. For those who believe, the Resurrection is always but a moment away.

My dearest Mother, allow me to keep vigil with you as you waited in perfect hope for the Resurrection of your divine Son. Help me to understand the beauty of every virtue alive in your Immaculate Heart. Help me to understand that the suffering you endured brought forth the perfection of virtue in your life, especially the virtue of divine hope.

My dear Mother, pray for me that I may be open to the promises of your Son in my life. Pray that I may hear Him speak to me and reveal His perfect plan. May I trust in that plan, even when all earthly hope seems lost. May I follow your own Immaculate example and trust in your dear Son always.

My resting Lord, as You lay in the tomb that Holy Saturday, You filled the heart of Your dear mother with an abundance of hope as she awaited the fulfillment of Your promise. You also promise me, and all who believe, that the sufferings of life are not the end. Your Resurrection is before me, and You promise to transform my life and the lives of all who trust in You. Give me the grace I need to keep vigil with Your dear mother no matter what cross I face in life.

Mother Mary, pray for me. Jesus, I trust in You.

Prayers for Holy Week

For those who use this meditation book for Lent, the prayers that follow can be prayed for Holy Week.

Holy Thursday

My Most Precious Lord Jesus, this night You gathered with Your Apostles to share with them Your last meal. But this was no ordinary meal. This was the gift of Your most Sacred Body and Blood, soon to be broken and poured out on the Cross for the salvation of the world.

Allow me, dear Lord, to spend this night in prayer and meditation with You. After the meal, You invited Your Apostles to join You for one hour, to stay awake and keep vigil as You prepared for Your arrest. The Apostles fell asleep, leaving You in Your bitter agony alone.

I accept Your gentle invitation of love, dear Lord, to spend this night in vigil with You. May I enter Your Heart as it faced the coming persecution You were to endure for my sins. May I console Your Sacred Heart and know the love and mercy that flowed forth.

Lord, when I face the crosses of my own life, give me Your divine courage and strength to say "Yes" to the will of the Father. Your love for me is abundant and is perfect in every way. Help me to know that love, to embrace it and to allow it into my life.

I make my vigil with You this night, dear Lord. I love You. Help me to love You with all my heart. Jesus, I trust in You.

Good Friday

My Most Glorious and Suffering Lord, it is Your Hour. It is the Hour by which You conquered sin and death. It is the Hour for which You came into this world, taking on flesh so as to offer Your precious life for the salvation of the world.

May I be with You, dear Lord, in these moments of suffering and death. May I, like Your mother, John and Mary Magdalene, stand at the foot of the Cross, gazing upon the perfect Gift of Love.

My suffering Lord, may I see in Your Cross the most perfect act ever known in this world. May I see Love in its purest form. May my eyes and soul look beyond the blood and pain and see Your divine Heart, pouring forth mercy upon me and upon the whole world.

Today I kneel in silent adoration of You, my God. I sit quietly, beholding the great mystery of our faith. I behold God, beaten, bruised, mocked, tortured and killed. But in this act, I see all grace and mercy flowing from Your wounded Heart. Bathe the world in Your mercy, dear Lord. Cover us with Your grace and draw us to new life through Your death. I love You, dear Lord. I love You with all my heart. Jesus, I trust in You.

Holy Saturday

My Lord, today all is silent. You have given Your precious life for the salvation of the world. You died a horrific death, poured out all mercy from Your wounded Heart, and now You rest in peace in the tomb as the soldiers keep vigil.

Lord, may I also keep vigil with You as You sleep. I know that this day ends with Your glorious triumph, Your victory over sin and death. But for now I sit quietly mourning Your death.

Help me, dear Lord, to enter into the sorrow and the silence of this Holy Saturday. Today no Sacraments are celebrated. Today the world waits in mourning in anticipation of the glory of new life!

As I keep vigil, awaiting the celebration of Your Resurrection, fill me with hope. Help me to look forward to the celebration of Your Resurrection, but also to look forward to the hope of my own share in the new life You won for the world. I entrust my whole being to You, dear Lord, as You lay lifeless and still. May Your rest transform the brokenness of my own soul, my weaknesses, my sin and my frailty. You are glorious and You bring the greatest good out of Your apparent defeat. I trust in Your power to do all things and I entrust my life to You. Jesus, I trust in You.

Easter

Halleluia! All glory, praise and honor to You, Most Glorious Lord Jesus! You have risen from the grave, You have conquered sin and death, You have opened the gates to Heaven! Halleluia! All praise and honor to You, Most Glorious Lord Jesus!

My Lord, hope is restored, joy and excitement are instilled in many hearts, as You quietly, gently and gloriously rise from the dead and bring forth new life for this fallen world. Sweet Jesus, give me the eyes of faith that I may see and believe in Your Resurrection. Help me to know the effects of Your triumph in my life. As I come to know You, my Resurrected Lord, help me to entrust to You all that I am and all that I hope to be. Help me to trust in the abundant mercy that flows from Your resurrected soul.

Dear Lord, help me to enter deeply into the mystery of Easter during this eight day celebration of the Octave of Easter. I pray that every day of this Octave will be a day of deepening trust and union with You in the glory of Your Resurrection.

Lord of Mercy, as our Church prepares for the glorious celebration of mercy, poured out in a special way on the eighth day of this Octave, on Divine Mercy Sunday, help me to open my heart more deeply than ever before to the abundance of grace and mercy You wish to bestow. Pour forth Your mercy into my life and into the lives of all Your children. I offer You my family, friends, community and the entire world. I pray for the faithful, the sinner, the lost and confused, the clergy, our Holy Father and all of Your precious children. May we all anticipate, with eager hope, the abundance of grace You wish to dispense.

My Resurrected Jesus of Mercy, I trust in You. Jesus, I trust in You. Jesus, I trust in You!

Halleluia! All glory, praise and honor to You, Most Glorious Lord Jesus! You have risen from the grave, You have conquered sin and death, You have opened the gates to Heaven! Halleluia! All praise and honor to You, Most Glorious Lord Jesus!

Additional Books from *My Catholic Life!*

Catholic Daily Reflections Series:

The *Catholic Daily Reflections Series* offers daily reflections and prayers based on the Gospel of the day. It is made up of four books covering the entire liturgical year. The books in this series are as follows:

> Vol. 1: *Advent and Christmas*
>
> Vol. 2: *Lent and Easter*
>
> Vol. 3: *Ordinary Time: Weeks 1-17*
>
> Vol. 4: *Ordinary Time: Weeks 18-34*

Daily Reflections on Divine Mercy: 365 Days with Saint Faustina

Short daily reflections and prayers for every day of the year sharing the wisdom of the Mercy of God as revealed in the *Diary* of Saint Faustina.

My Catholic Life! Series:

For a complete summary of the Catholic Faith, as contained in the *Catechism of the Catholic Church*, see the three volume summary of our faith:

> Vol. 1: *My Catholic Faith! Summary of Catholic Doctrine*
>
> Vol. 2: *My Catholic Worship! Summary of Sacraments & Prayer*
>
> Vol. 3: *My Catholic Morals! Summary of Catholic Morality*

All writings, reflections and prayers from *My Catholic Life!* are available free of charge by using our *Catholic Daily Reflections* Android and iOS mobile app. Visit your app store today to download for free.

All of the content of these books and app are available at: <u>www.myCatholic.Life</u>

Notes:

Made in the USA
Coppell, TX
19 March 2020

17119111R00079